The Star Keys

Living Beyond 2012
In The Age of The Gods

Also by Walter Starcke:

THE GOSPEL OF RELATIVITY

THE DOUBLE THREAD

THE ULTIMATE REVOLUTION

HOMESICK FOR HEAVEN

IT'S ALL GOD

THE THIRD APPEARANCE

JOEL GOLDSMITH & I

To be published in 2012:

THE DAILY VOICE

For more information on CDs, Newsletters,
and workshops contact:
The Guadalupe Press
www.walterstarcke.com
Erons@www.walterstarcke.com

The Star Keys
Living Beyond 2012 In The Age of The Gods

Walter & Eron Starcke

Guadalupe Press
2012

GUADALUPE PRESS

Boerne, Texas

The Guadalupe Press
P.O. Box 865
Boerne, Texas 78006
www.walterstarcke.com

Starcke, Walter H.
Spiritual Globalization
The Star Keys
Living Beyond 2012 in the Age of The Gods
by Walter Starcke & Eron Starcke
1. Spiritual 2. Mysticism 3. New World Age
4. Consciousness Studies

ISBN
978-0-929845-12-8

Book & Cover Design by
Eron Howell-Starcke

FORWARD

My life has been about the coming of age of the evolving state of consciousness that has ushered in a New Age. Now we are living in the transition between two cycles as 2012 marks the beginning of what the Mayans knew would be the Age of The Gods. We have been the forerunners and the first to step into that true New Age, even as so many cling to the old. This transition began over 2,000 years ago and is a process that will continue to evolve, as we realize we are multi-dimensional beings living in the Age of Gods.

As I write this book, I am drifting between dimensions. As the veil becomes thin I realize it is imperative that further clarifications to a state of consciousness set forth in my book, IT'S ALL GOD, be shared during this critical time. Eron, my wife and partner for over 30 years, is helping to clarify my messages and bring them into awareness so that they will live far beyond and be useful to those following the path. I am blessed with this time of transition between what appears to be life and death. As never before I realize Life is eternal as the tethers that hold me in human form loosen. I can still enjoy the world, smile as I sit in the hot sunshine, savor a glass of wine, and hold Eron's hand. We are here to do that, enjoy the process of creation as we create Love in expression in infinite ways.

As the veil lifts around me, time and space elude me, my consciousness is free to cross into the mystical realms. I am Homesick for Heaven. Words and sentences become a jumble of sticks, yet Love does not fade. Love sustains me, Love bridges my consciousness with Eron's so that she can write the words to clarify the pathway into expanded living. My life is and was perfect, every step up or down, as your lives are each perfect. Whether I am in this body or a Lighter Body of radiant energy, I am with you. And I love you.

We all stand at the doorway to freedom beyond limitations, to life everlasting, to creating as God – delightfully, intentionally, subjectively, infinitely worlds beyond worlds.

Enjoy the Divine Process.

TABLE OF CONTENTS

INTRODUCTION

I have no desire to invent a new philosophy or religion or to refute any that presently exist. I feel that everyone is attending the right church, studying the right teaching, and learning the lessons they are ready to learn in the process of discovering what works for them in their present state of consciousness. Everyone is being led by an invisible hand.
Walter Starcke, IT'S ALL GOD

This invisible hand is the Omnipresent, Omniscient, and Omnipotent Divine Process. I have lived a long productive life, and to the best of my ability I have communicated the Truths that have become realized in my awareness. I find it interesting that each of my books has had a theme, a catchy phrase, or title that motivated and focused my mind during the writing of each book. This new book started out to be about "Spiritual Globalization" but the Divine Process has taken over. Little did I know that the phrase "Double Thread" that was given to me so long ago would hold the Star Keys to living beyond 2012 as Gods on Earth. The *Double Thread* Process has lead me from both the within and without into the exploration of consciousness. Now it is with ever-greater clarity that I share the fruits of this journey with you.

As never before I understand that there is only one Truth – detailed in its infinity, yet simple in its clarity. In this book we will state the Truth clearly from my experience in exploring Higher Consciousness and applying that consciousness to my daily life. More importantly, I know as never before, that to live beyond 2012 we must live in and as the awareness of Universal Truth. Life as we have known it will end; this has to be to free us to live in the Age of the Gods.

Mystics and metaphysicians from the past, including Jesus, have presented the Truth in ways that could be received at the time, but the Truth contained within often needed clarification as human consciousness grew in understanding. If you could see my BIBLE, it's underlined, scribbled in and corrected on almost every page. In IT'S ALL GOD, hopefully I clarified and helped to reconcile the Judeo-Christian traditions that helped form the concepts and beliefs that have created our present state of affairs, and helped prepare a way forward.

Each of my books is a stepping-stone along the path of awareness offered to those who are also on the path. The awareness in each one was perfect for that point in the journey. Whether you have followed me thus far or have just picked up this book, you are standing at the door to a true New Age. The Keys to unlocking that door are already at hand.

I'm not trying to rattle cages, win friends and influence people, get rich, or build a following. At this point I'm ready to make the transition from living in a body to a pure Spirit Being without its physical limitations. In the future, humanity will be able to live in the Kingdom of Heaven on Earth beyond limitations. Consciousness, which is my life, is eternal, yet is evolving rapidly.

My work is about trusting this Process. Eron and I share this Process that we have trusted to lead us to this shift in consciousness. It is our life. Together we offer you our consciousness and that of The Spirit that flows through and as That that we are.

As Walter was writing HOMESICK FOR HEAVEN *and began to get new messages that would lead to the* IT'S ALL GOD *material, I wrestled with a huge piece of the puzzle of awakening consciousness – God. I couldn't figure "God" out; I couldn't find a place for a God in my belief system. I tried, I wrestled, I meditated. But no God spoke to me. As I shared my frustrations with Walter, he shared his changing perspective that it's all God. Then click, this realization that it's all God, was life changing. God wasn't outside, God wasn't a thing, God is all. God is both my Higher Consciousness, and Divine Higher Consciousness; God is totally all, including the experience of our life.*

This concept went beyond all former concepts of God that had passed through my consciousness and reconciled a state of consciousness beyond words. The new puzzle pieces clicked in old Buddhist ones, clarified outmoded Christian ones, and spoke to me from my own Infinite Self. Without this step I could not have moved forward.

In many languages and religions a major sign post reads, "It's All God", taking it leads to the awareness of inclusive expanded consciousness. As time has passed our realization that all consciousness is evolving beyond old concepts has become an amazing journey into the freedom of Truth.

We invite you one this journey of freedom.

Eron Starcke

THE NEW BOOK

I awoke this morning with the clear thought impressed upon my consciousness, that we must now go beyond the knowing that "It's All God." We do not need to rewrite that book, yet I do understand that at some point we must all take this step for it is the pivotal realization that has led up to this new cycle of consciousness and will make it possible to step into the future and live beyond 2012 as *Global Spiritual God Beings.*

From this awareness there is still further to go in the realization of this Truth to enable us to live as the Divine Beings that we are. It is time to awaken into the new cycle long predicted – as the Mayans called it "The Age of the Gods." Now we are exploring life beyond limitations created by outdated concepts.

I heard that we are to make the Truth as simple, direct, and accessible as possible. It is not complicated; in fact it becomes simpler with understanding. All consciousness is a "work in progress," subject to future review. As never before, Eron and I understand the need to be free from past moral and philosophical judgments, to let go of all limiting concepts of good and evil, in favor of trusting the forward, uplifting flow of the Divine All-inclusive Process.

The realization that it's all God has led us to the necessity of becoming active participants in shifting the current crisis of consciousness that rattles and shakes the earth and all our foundations. All together as humans, we have jumped into "Free Fall." And the whole world is going with us. The step into being the fullness of Divine/Human expression is a leap into letting go of boundaries, limitations, and old paradigms. It is a leap into the space of subjective consciousness – a space that only appears to be empty, but is far from it. In truth it is the step into the All-ness of higher vibrational consciousness – the consciousness of the vibration of Love.

Economic crisis is global, just as is the environmental crisis that threatens to destroy the earth as we have known it. Flares of fear-based consciousness try in vain to fight against imagined enemies. Everywhere we are faced with the necessity of a change that must come from a shift in consciousness that moves our priorities from the objective to the subjective alignment with natural order. It is no accident that we are now traveling through the center of the Milky Way on a new 26,000-year cycle of quantum awakening.

We are truly led by an invisible hand, *The Process.* Join us on this amazing journey into the true New Age.

To Set the Stage

We stand at the beginning of a True New Age as we move into a new 26,000-year cycle the Mayans called the Age of the Gods. Humanity has been on a long journey of expanding consciousness and is now emerging from a cycle where the predominant focus of consciousness was on objective effects as cause rather than on the true subjective nature of the Universe. Our lives have been governed by objective laws rather than spiritual principles. It's time to get our priorities straight. It is time to become fully aware, Spiritual Beings not only connected globally but cosmically.

Every 5,125 years we enter a new earth cycle. In 2012 we came to the end of a cycle that began in approximately 3,114 B.C. and the beginning of a new great cycle that heralds a tremendous shift in consciousness. These repeating cycles were foretold by ancient mystics of the Hopi, Mayan, and Hindu traditions, as well as many others. Greg Braden has written a detailed account of these cycles and their meanings in his book, FRACTAL TIME.

Braden explains that the Mayan calendar is unique among the world's timekeepers because it is "the single most accurate system of tracking nature's cycles of galaxies, planets, and our relationship to the sun known until the 20th century." Without modern technology, they knew that the current cycle is the fifth 5,125-year cycle of the earth's precession in a 25,625 year journey through the 12 constellations of the zodiac.

The movement of the sun into alignment with the equator of the Milky Way marks a long journey of cosmic significance that reflects our evolution in awakening consciousness. Life on Earth will not end, rather it enters a period of great opportunity to take a leap in awareness and evolution.

Braden explains the Hopi prophecy which tells of our choice on this journey:

> *The life plan exists as a simple map holding a profound message, and that it's preserved on a rock face in northern Arizona's Hopi village of Oraibi – a place called Prophecy Rock. What makes this map so unusual is that it's not a conventional one of places. Instead, it's a map of "being," of consciousness. It tells us the state of consciousness that's required to survive the great changes that accompany the end of our age.*

In it we see two paths that lead to the new world age of the fifth world. Each leads to a very different experience. The lower path shows people healthy and vital, living to advanced ages and harvesting corn from an abundant field. The upper one depicts people as well; a closer look however, shows that their heads aren't attached to their bodies and are floating just above their shoulders. The line beneath them is rough and jagged. These people used their minds instead of choosing the spiritual path.

The good news is that the map also shows a third path, a vertical line connects the jagged and the smooth ones. This line is said to represent the ladder of choice.

Whether the transition between cycles is rough or smooth, we will be on a new path of our own choosing. This is the time for us to step forward into being Globalized, Spiritual Beings living by the realizations of the Star Keys beyond old outmoded judgments and limiting belief systems.

The shift is a long process, a journey through consciousness. We are entering a new cycle of continually repeating cycles; spirals of consciousness expressing multi–dimensionally. We are not who we were 5,125 years ago, nor as we will be even a few hundred years in the future, as evolving consciousness has quickened our vibrations of manifestation. We have choices to make and actions to take. It does not have to be hard; there are guideposts and Star Keys to follow.

Trust the Process.

Grab your hat; the Star Keys are in hand, let's get going.

Chapter One

The Two Keys & Two Stumbling Blocks

As I promised, let me say this simply and right up front as we start this process together:

The First Star Key is the realization that it's all God – To know God as unlimited, all-inclusive subjective Source, the One Power and One Cause.

In order to save the earth and all who live here, there must be a shift in consciousness of such proportions that the scales are tipped from disharmony to harmony. To do this we must become consciously aware of the two underlying Truths of the Universe and use them to help us make this shift in consciousness.

As human consciousness expands in awareness, it realizes that it's true subjective nature is Cause. The shift happens as one realizes the First Star Key that there is one Infinite Source of all in all. This knowledge, when it becomes our predominant consciousness, unlocks the flow of unlimited possibilities. It allows our subjective awareness to melt the objective illusions of ethnicity, nationality, and all fear based thoughts that divide and pit man against man and humanity against nature.

To move into the Age of the Gods, first we must "Seek the Kingdom of God." This literally means to dwell in subjective consciousness of Divine Mind. We must know God as our infinite subjective Source.

To know God as unlimited, all-inclusive subjective Source, we must let go of any concept of God that is less than All. This all-inclusive, subjective state of being allows the infinite Creative Source of All to flow freely, impersonally, in natural order. This is Kingdom Consciousness.

Kingdom Consciousness experiences God beyond objective thought as Omnipotence, Omnipresence, and Omniscience. Our concept of God must go beyond any limiting belief system; for some this might mean letting go of the word "God" in favor of a more encompassing phrase like Divine Source, or Infinite Mind, or Infinite Creative Source. Eron prefers these; however, I know what I mean when I say the word, "God," and do not limit my concept. Therefore, in this book I will mostly use the term God and now you will know what I mean when I do.

The Second Star Key is the self-realization of The Presence of God as individual expression.

At the personal level nothing comes in singles, or absolutes. There are always two necessary directions to take on any path. Just as in the Two Commandments Jesus gave, one direction lies in the love of God, which is to say the concept of God one entertains, and the other in one's love of, or attitude toward the neighbor or material side of life, thus the double Keys.

> *You shall love the Lord your God with all your heart, with all your soul, and with all your mind. This the greatest and first commandment. The second resembles it: You shall love your neighbor as your self.* Mt. 22:37–39

Kingdom Consciousness must also contain the Second Key – **we are the Presence of Infinite Source personalized.** With the shift in consciousness, we understand that there is no separate "neighbor" rather there is one Body of Christ, God in individual expression.

God is not separate from Its creations.

As long as God is considered to be other than our own individual consciousness our entire belief system is false.

God is in no way something that is other than and apart from our consciousness.

Any thought of God as other than that which is inherent in our individual makeup is a lie.

The recognition and awareness of Infinite Divine Consciousness is the first priority and with that in consciousness the Word is made flesh in material terms. When that happens, the flesh reflects the perfection of consciousness, and we move into Kingdom living in the Age of the Gods. These two truths are the Star Keys to living beyond 2012. Neither are complete in themselves; to both we add the complement of Love.

THE CAUSE OF CONFUSION

There are two stumbling blocks that are on our path as we move toward this awareness. They reflect the double nature of the Keys.

The stumbling blocks are the contradiction in our concept of God, and the misconception of our own individual being.

To move past these blocks you have to pass through the unknowing of our preconceived judgments and beliefs. In other words you have to "unknow" what you think you know and know anew.

After years of trying to eliminate my sense of separation from the divine as well as to overcome bouts of personal anxiety, I realized what it was that I had to "unknow." Instead of trying to put spiritual salve on mental sores, I discovered what the initial source of my past confusions had been. Like it or not, we are all conditioned by the interpretations of religious, moral, and social concepts that have been passed on to us from birth. Many of these have become stumbling blocks to higher awareness because of their limiting concepts. Our goal now is to become free of judgments in order to discover the misconceptions that have plagued us ever since we bought into accustomed interpretations. I can not stress to you enough how important it is to be able to know that there is further to go along the path.

To begin to fully understand that all is God, Source, Infinite Consciousness, we must let go of the beliefs that limit our awareness and thus our forward progress. This is hard to do on the level of mind. Joel Goldsmith would say, "You can't solve a problem on the level of the problem." More to the point, Albert Einstein said, "No problem can be solved from the same level of consciousness that created it."

The problem is that our conscious mind is the center for self-awareness, but only controls about 5% of our lives. This mind can think that it is in control, say affirmations, think positively, even be creative, and make spontaneous changes, but our lives are actually controlled by our perceptions which are the beliefs we hold locked in our sub-conscious mind.

Bruce Lipton explains in his ground breaking book, BIOLOGY OF BELIEF:

> *The subconscious mind process 20,000,000 environmental stimuli per second v. 40 environmental stimuli interpreted by the conscious mind in the same second...The subconscious mind is the most powerful information processor known...*

The subconscious mind holds onto concepts as hard and fast judgments that dictate our manifest life, not to mention limiting our spiritual awareness. In fact, our whole perception of God as being Infinite Creative Source, or Infinite Mind, is limited by objective judgment in the mind. That mind cannot hold onto the concept of infinite, creative, abundant, impersonal Love as Source. That mind wants to hold on to a concept of God from which we limit our ability to express creative Source. That mind wants to hold on to a God that will be a protector Father to save it from self-created fears. These fears arise from our observed lack of control of our conscious mind. We often think that we are helpless victims of the outer world. But we are not.

To be a fully conscious being, these limitations have to be released so that one may have the capacity to be simultaneously aware of objective physical appearances while realizing one's spiritual significance and relationship to the Divine Whole.

To move into the Age of the Gods, we must pass through the door of letting go of limiting beliefs and move into the unknown. When I say, "to be fully conscious," I am referring to a state of being aware that is a mystical experience of Being.

As Bruce Lipton discovered, "our beliefs control our biology." When we let go of limiting beliefs held in the vast subconscious mind, we are able to "change old responses any time we desire."

We agree with many evolutionary scientists who now believe consciousness has evolved over the ages and exists in various stages through out an infinite number of organisms, including humans. In humans, consciousness becomes aware of its own complexity. As this state of consciousness evolves into being super conscious, we move into the Age of the Gods. Mystics have led the way by experiencing the true nature of Being through meditation. We must become fully conscious to be Global Spiritual Beings living and thriving beyond 2012.

In one of my books, I referred to the mystical experience as passing through the "cloud of unknowing." It took decades to glimpse at the experience of going beyond "knowing," in which one goes beyond the confusing self-created puzzles of the mind. There is an old Zen saying, "Paradox and confusion are the two fierce guardians at the gateway to the truth of who you are."

So take heart, if you have also been beset by the puzzles of paradox and confusion, you are at the door of the process of a great shift in consciousness. In THE BOOK OF NOT KNOWING by Peter Ralston, the author explores the paradox that evolving consciousness arises not from what is known, but from the state of "not-knowing." His book is a long in-depth read, but is perhaps the "Bible" of Consciousness.

> *Not-knowing is itself. It is primary. Before knowing can happen, there must first be a space for it, a state of non-knowing. In our culture that doesn't matter – we avoid not-knowing. We avoid the appearance of it, the awareness of it, the existence of it as a primary state of being. You and I continually experience not-knowing, but our attention is on what we know and perceive, so we don't discern – and don't want to discern – the not knowing. Although not-knowing is the "source" of all knowing and is indispensable for creativity, it remains a virtually unrecognized principle in our culture.*
> Peter Ralston, THE BOOK OF NOT KNOWING

To have the experience of passing through the cloud of unknowing, we must create a space that is an open pathway for our super conscious Mind to over-ride limitations with the creative energies of unconditioned thought that flow directly from the Mind of Divine Source.

When the super conscious Mind overrides outmoded concepts hidden in the sub conscious, it allows the power of our own creative will to create anew. It is in this state beyond known concepts that true creativity takes place. It is the space where inspiration flows directly from Infinite Source into our individual awareness. It's where Einstein received insights, Michelangelo saw his sculptures, and Jesus touched the flow of the Christ Mind.

The super conscious Mind is the Divine Mind, and thus the Christ Mind. Through the mystical experience, we can clear a way through our judgments and old beliefs to live from our super conscious Mind that realizes it is one with God.

We must literally change our minds. As we move into this new cycle, we will be able to access deeper (albeit higher) states of consciousness. As Jesus foretold, we will do greater things than those of the past.

In the new Age of the Gods, miracles will become daily activities. In fact, miracles will no longer be miracles; they will be a way of life.

Later in this book, we will explore ways in which we can listen to that Mind and free ourselves to be intentional creators who are aware of their Divinity and act from Divine Source. As you can see, we are asking you to change some long held human concepts. We will not need them in the new cycle. Our outmoded limiting concept of God denies that it's all God, the flowers and the fertilizer. To free ourselves from these limitations we must experience the subjective Mind of God.

As THE COURSE IN MIRACLES instructs us, we must see with the "eyes of God." This is the mystical experience beyond words that carries one into multidimensional worlds and cuts the tethers and ropes of judgment.

The mystical experience sees Omnipotence, Omnipresence, and Omniscience not as three separate energies but three different viewpoints or dimensions of One Energy or Being-ness. The mystics are right, we are living a life, not of time or space, but as Spirit, which knows no time, no distance, and no boundaries.

The way in which our own consciousness unfolds dictates the quality of our physical and human experience.

TWO APPROACHES:
THE SUBJECTIVE & OBJECTIVE

There are two basic approaches to the way we function as human beings. Both are necessary and both are equally valuable. We either judge life objectively in terms of and by relating to its visible material appearances, or subjectively, in terms of its invisible values and purposes. Together they represent our consciousness. It has been a long, long journey trying to arrive objectively, step-by-step to an awareness of the subjective truths symbolized by what we see. The mystical approach is the process of becoming aware that the subjective nature of a thing or situation is the Cause that created its objectified presence.

Until now the objective way of evaluating life has predominantly assumed top priority while the subjective, symbolic, or spiritual importance of what we see has been of secondary importance. **Ultimately we must shift our priorities from the objective to the subjective. It is only on this subjective level of Cause that we can change the world.**

Once we perceive the creative nature of consciousness, our priorities begin to shift from focusing on the material side of life to realizing the importance of subjective harmony and joy as our natural state of Being.

As we align our priorities with Source our creations are more harmonious, loving, and joyous.

This alignment with Source is the First Star Key: *The realization that it's all God – To know God as unlimited, all-inclusive subjective Source, One Power and One Cause.*

The Second Key is its' double nature: *The self-realization of The Presence of God as individual expression. Thus the Second Key is God manifesting as individual form.*

As we move into the New Age our priorities will shift from seeing our neighbor as separate or even as an evil enemy, from using economic pressure to get results, from reacting to our self created fears as our cultures crumble. These are all objective priorities that currently dominate our autopilot minds. **When we solve this crisis of where and how we view life and realize that a subjective approach fosters the love of fellow humans, and encourages international co-operation, there will be no more wars.**

Yes, that's right, in the Age of The Gods there will be no more wars.

By subjectively becoming aware of the consciousness of a situation before taking action at the objective level, we can be masters of our own destinies. All creations are made on the subjective level. All change is made on the subjective level. Try as we have, we have not fought the war to end all wars. We cannot solve the problem on the level of the problem! Fighting yet another war against our separated objectified neighbor only creates more separation.

We can use the First Star Key to turn subjectively to the realization that God is All. It is the Key that unlocks Infinite Source to flow into all situations to restore harmony.

The Second Star Key heals the false concept of separation from our neighbor. When we view our neighbor as separate, they might have something we do not or take something that we have and we become fearful. As we hold the Second Key, we know there is no separate neighbor, because we are All One with that Infinite Source. As one with Source, our subjective consciousness is one with all the creative, infinite energy of the universe, so how can we lack anything? This shift in consciousness will end all wars.

All our manifestations, even our own physical bodies are the direct result of our consciousness manifesting. As we move into expanded awareness, we must shift from limiting objective judgments to dwell first in the harmony of Infinite Invisible Cause. This can only happen in the space of unknowing beyond old concepts that imprison and limit our lives. As we evolve into greater awareness, our subjective consciousness deliberately manifests freely from unlimited Source.

All is Infinite Mind (Consciousness) and its infinite manifestation. That principle became the underlying foundation of the whole metaphysical movement – a movement based primarily on a subjective experience of life that, in turn, would manifest objectively as a more healthy and harmonious way of living.

This shift in awareness from an objective way of looking at life into a subjective approach may sound speculative, but in order to understand the evolution of our spiritual consciousness and to discover how this non-material viewpoint can affect our lives in our day-to-day existence, we have to become aware of a whole new way of perceiving ourselves.

THE MIND IS A TOOL

When early metaphysicians found that through positive thinking and what they called mental "treatment" they could change conditions, many fell into the trap of making a God out of the mind itself. In the process they dehumanized themselves. Fortunately, the intellect is no longer being endowed with Divinity in the way that it was in the past. The mind is more a depository of facts rather than a decision maker. How we perceive those facts is consciousness as mover. Until we understand the purpose and function of the mind, what it means for us to use the mind as co-creators under the direction of our Higher Consciousness will be misunderstood.

For instance, we ordinarily think of the mind objectively as a thinking instrument even though its real purpose is subjective. The mind should be understood to be a "seeing" instrument, an instrument of vision that we use to turn perception or intuition into knowing.

As a mental instrument it interprets the conditions that Spirit or consciousness creates. The conscious or sub-conscious activity of the mind translates our perceptions into material reality.

As such, the mind is not a power. It's a tool. We need it in the same way Michelangelo needed a chisel. He couldn't scratch the Pieta out of a piece of dense marble with his finger nails, but to believe that his mind was the power rather than his consciousness is a false belief that confuses perception with thought.

Thinking is quantitative – it defines the shape and size of what it reflects upon.

Perception is qualitative, which is to say that the situations resulting from our perceptions reflect the values inherent in our consciousness.

One can imitate or reproduce with the mind, but original creativity is an action of Spirit. First comes vision, consciousness, intuition, or Spirit, and all use the mind to turn perception into material reality.

Again, to receive inspirations from Infinite Mind, we have to open to that space of not-knowing that allows for possibilities of creation to become concepts that are formed in the mind. In other words, we have to let go of our preconceived beliefs, our judgments, and our conditioned concepts, to create a space of open receptivity. We don't have to abandon all that has made us who we think we are humanly, but we have to suspend the hold these concepts have on our mental process.

We have to create the space of unknowing for Infinite Mind to flow and experience new possibilities beyond our wildest imagination. This is the New Mind of the Gods living in the next great cycle.

Years ago, a man came to see me wanting to know about meditation and its purpose. I asked him what profession he was in, and he said that he was a harbor-dredging engineer. I asked him how he did his job. He explained that when he was called to propose a solution to a problem he gathered in all the facts and decided what should be done. I said, "Wait a minute. After you get all the facts, isn't there then a moment when you pause before making choices? Don't you listen and let your intuition speak?" To my delight, the man responded, "Ah, then meditation is that moment when I make space for my summations to crystallize."

Yes, the mystical or meditative experience is the "space" between what is objectively known. It is the space of our creative, subjective Self.

We use the mind to accumulate the facts, but then we intuit our actions no matter how simple or how complicated our goals.

Facts are objective, but intuition – inner knowing – is subjective.

IF I BE LIFTED UP

Except for a few among us, up until now, everything has been taken objectively, even seemingly spiritual statements. For instance, when Jesus said, "And when I am lifted up from the earth, I will draw everyone to myself," it was interpreted to mean that he, a man, would physically attract all other men to him personally. Subjectively it is impersonal and entirely different. It means all humanity will be lifted up into Kingdom Consciousness.

Jesus followed in a long tradition of Kabalistic mystics who spoke with the fluid words of mystical interpretation. Subjectively Jesus was saying that if he rose to Christ Consciousness he would be aware that there was one Self that included all. If we lift our consciousness into the Infinite Source of all life we refer to as God, we know we are one with all others – thus all are lifted up. Using the Star Keys, Jesus set a pathway for us all.

> Fr. Richard Rhor says of Jesus:
> *To understand Jesus in a whole new way, you must first know that Christ is not his last name, but the pre-existent Christ Consciousness that existed from all eternity (Colossians 1:15-20) and his omnipresent identity after the Resurrection– which now includes humanity and all of creation along with it (Ephesians 1:9-11). Jesus became the Christ (Acts 2:36), by his own process of transformation, and now wonderfully includes us in this sweeping, historical, and victorious identity!*

It may sound simplistic or exaggerated, but the subjective interpretation of Jesus' statement is that as he lifted up his consciousness he would see his oneness with all else; and because he is One with All, all will then be lifted up into this awareness. By doing so he was preparing us for Spiritual Globalization.

Globalization will reach its fulfillment, perhaps in the distant future, when all those on earth realize we are interconnected in a way that makes all beings members of one global family.

We, as we are lifted up, will be conscious that we are one with all beings. It is all God.

THE CREATOR YOU

OK, here we go into more detailed clarifications. The thinking mind cannot wrap itself around the subject of mysticism or descriptions of the mystical experience, much less Omnipotence, Omnipresence, and Omniscience. It can only register the various concepts and deposit them in the subconscious. That is as far as our human intellect can go. Nevertheless, mentally formulating and repeating the possibility of having an "other world" experience has its value. Once registered in the subconscious, concepts of our spiritual potential can hibernate and one day birth an actual mystical experience, often when least expected.

The inner experience cannot be activated by mental effort, so the best we can do is read the words and allow the possibility of an opening in consciousness to what is unknown.

When it is time, we will be led through the clouds of unknowing to a new opening in the consciousness of infinite possibilities.

Modern science's great contribution has not so much been that it has led to the invention of incredible technology, but rather what it has accomplished by opening the doorways of previously unrecognized possibilities.

I would say that in my scientific and philosophical work, my main concern has been with understanding the nature of reality in general and of consciousness in particular as a coherent whole, which is never static or complete but which is an unending process of movement and unfoldment.
David. Bohm, WHOLENESS AND THE IMPLICATE ORDER

When quantum physicists announced that invisible consciousness manifests visible forms, and that everything we see symbolizes the consciousness that created it, they affirmed what the mystics of all time have claimed but been unable to prove. Science has revealed that we humans are not just physical beings but creativity itself. By revealing consciousness as the invisible Cause of all that exists, it has exposed the concept of a personalized God as the Creator.

Despite the fact that the Scripture says that in the beginning "is the Word and the Word is made flesh," it took science to show us that the spiritual self and the physical self are one in that the creation is the child of the Creator. One is the Cause, the idea or Word, and the other is the effect, the material flesh.

Creations never leave Source. Creation and Cause are One.

The interpretation of the universe from the standpoint of its causative Principle, whereby thought looks out from instead of up to Mind, is emerging. A new and spiritual basis states that being is one infinite, indivisible whole consisting of an infinite coordination of ideas that emanate from the one Infinite Mind and are amenable to their Principle alone. Not surprisingly, physics echoes this statement in finding that beneath the apparently random behavior of particles, governed by no higher a law than probability, is a deep and underlying harmony. One physicist, Dr. Andrews of Johns Hopkins University has described this as "the music of the spheres." John Hargreaves, As "I" SEE It

To live a creative and successful life:
It is of paramount importance for each of us to be aware of the difference between our two selves and understand from which end of the telescope we are viewing our lives at any given moment.
Remember there is but **One Life and One Power in the Universe, God.**
Know the First Star Key – realizing that all-inclusive God is the Source of all as subjective Cause.
God is Consciousness; Consciousness is the Creator.

In saying that we are made in the image of God, we are acknowledging that we are primarily the creator of our physical bodies and all that appears in our lives. That which we create is not primarily who we are, but rather it is that which we as Divine Beings have created. In this respect our bodies are not us; they are the product of our creative energy focused through our consciousness. Yet the created never leaves its source, just as the wave does not leave the ocean.

We are Consciousness. The music of the spheres lives us as the sound vibrations of our lives.

Because we create our bodies, it is as though our bodies are our children. As parents we have the responsibility of taking care of our bodies, but to be effective, we must do so without believing we are the body.

In the process we must keep from once more starting to believe that we are our bodies rather than that which has created, maintains, and sustains them.

When we absorb and are consciously aware that we are the creator of our bodies, we will no longer believe that we are only what we see in the mirror – that which aches, pains, and imprisons us in the belief that we are confined to a limited material world. Though it doesn't make sense to the rational mind, just knowing that, lessens the control our bodies have over us. We can then be freer to create our physical form to live in harmony.

The door to freedom begins when we accept the possibility that at those times when our physical manifestations falter, we, as creators, have given them the power to do so.

However, there is no need for us to feel guilty about this. We live in a seemingly dualistic world, and the flip side of the coin of pain and tiredness can turn out to be a blessing. It can be if we allow ourselves to see those difficulties as signals telling us that we are once more believing that we are our bodies, rather than that our bodies are ours.

Personally, it is easier for me to be able to separate myself from seeing myself as my body, and for me to be able to take a look at it as its being my creation if I close my eyes. Then when I stand aside and in my mind's eye envision the part of my body that is faltering, I can do something about it. I can remember that I am the Creator and thereby remove the belief that my physical condition has power on its own, thus I shine the light of my wholeness on it. After I have examined my physical presence and reclaimed my creative authority, I am better able to neutralize the condition. Eron would say that this is "Seeing with the eyes of God," as it explains in A COURSE IN MIRACLES. It is exactly that, shifting our seeing awareness to our Divine Subjective perspective rather than our limited physical eyes that see the objective world.

Because I have such a profound belief that there is but One Power and One Presence appearing as my individual being, when a problem persists I do not feel that I am a failure for having it. Instead, I know that when whatever it is that is bothering me has served its Divine purpose as a wake-up call, it will reveal itself as a nothingness, a nothingness that I, as the only Creator, has lent power to.

As I said to begin with, it is almost impossible to believe that we are the creators of everything that appears in our lives, because every TV commercial proclaims that effects are cause and that they have the power to affect us. Social media tells us that to change our lives, we eat this or wear that, or rub this on our bodies. If we believe the lie of good and evil, we limit our ability to flow with harmony over rocks or down smooth streams. Even though the whole world reflects this huge outmoded concept of good and bad, right and wrong, we can stop being used by them if we are consciously aware that we are the creators of the whole spectrum of our lives.

As long as we look beyond the effects to the consciousness that created them, we can change that consciousness to change the form.

In other words, we live in an invisible world that creates the visible, and when we look to and trust that invisible creative being that we are, it visibly manifests heaven on earth. Actually, there is a simpler explanation that is even more difficult to accept because of its simplicity. Although there is consciousness in all things, we are different than other living beings because we have the power of imagination. We image everything from the moment we wake in the morning until we go to bed at night and what we image, we create. How different our lives would be if we controlled our images.

I began this section by saying that it is a concept the thinking mind cannot really accept. The answer is in the silence. **We can register the concept that we create all that is in our lives, but the only way we can activate that concept is by going beyond all concepts, which means in the silence.**

The silence is not a matter of sound. It is a silence of images, of thoughts, and of concepts. It is a nothingness, a no-thing-ness that opens the doorway of not-knowing to the Age of Knowing and being Gods. There too, we cannot achieve the silence by trying to stop the mind by the mind. However, **we can let thoughts pass through without resisting them, or holding to fixed, limiting judgments.**

Intent is the mother of creation; so if we quiet ourselves as much as possible and our intention (inner tension) is to enter a silence of Spirit we find that there it is all God.

Chapter Two

GOING BEYOND

BEYOND OUR MYTHS

In writing this book we wanted to explain things in every-day factual terms that would appeal to everyone, even those readers with an aversion to words that smack of theological implication. But we find that there is a reason we am unable to do so. **We can't go beyond what holds us within its boundaries.**

As we mentioned earlier, this is a stumbling block. We are never free until we come to terms with our cultural heritage. That doesn't mean we have to accept it in the way it has been handed down to us. But by the fact of our having been raised in a particular society, concepts may have been planted in our unconscious mind of which we might not even be aware. If we can look at our myths in a new way, freed of traditional interpretations, some of the old unconscious blockages can be flushed out.

Our Western culture has been shaped by the Judeo/Christian tradition that has stayed alive for so many years because there is a profound energy in some of the underlying truths that are tucked away in it. However, we don't want to leave old, falsely conditioned words festering in our unconscious minds as long as we can reinterpret them and better understand how certain distorted interpretations have impregnated our collective consciousness.

Exploring Oriental and other religions can add other perspectives and help clarify and make us aware of hidden meanings we have overlooked that exist in our own cultural religions, but in the end, we are never completely free until we have come to terms with the overall cultural concepts that have conditioned the Western society in which we live.

Personally, I have a debt of gratitude for my visits to the Vedanta monastery in the late 40s and early 50s. There Master Swami Prabvananda opened my eyes in a way that made it possible for me to appreciate the symbols of my background in a different light. Swami was extremely personal and made each one he met feel special. Tears of joy would come into his eyes when I came into his presence, and he made me feel not only loved but worthy of being loved. If I told him of my problems, he would listen, understand and connect so personally that the problems dwindled in importance. The feeling of Love that surrounded him made everything else disappear, at least for that moment.

Eron has explored the connections of Eastern concepts, which while expressed differently, echo the essential teachings of Jesus. We in the West often do not think of Eastern teachings as being on the same path of Love and Light, but the light of truth shines from many vantage points.

The Truths and Keys we are sharing in this book are true throughout the Universe, they are not exclusive to the western world. This will be a great eye-opener as we step into this new Age of Global Oneness.

> *When you realize that eternity is right here now, that it is within your possibility to experience the eternity of your own truth and being, then you grasp the following: That which you are was never born and will never die. All the Gods, all the heavens, all the hells, are within you.*
> Joseph Campbell THOU ART THAT: TRANSFORMING RELIGIOUS METAPHOR

From our perspective in the West, there are many stumbling blocks we have to go beyond, all-inherent in our cultural/religious traditions. The BIBLE had been our guidebook for the predominance of this cycle. The BIBLE has lost the dominant position. To a great extent, our universal media explosion, the ever-expanding Internet, and the plethora of e-books and print material that constantly compete for our attention, have preempted the BIBLE's importance for many – particularly the young.

It's just not the only book in town anymore. Up until the last century when radio, TV, and the movies became popular, the BIBLE was our cable television. It was our leading source of soap opera scandal and human-interest stories – a gold mine of social and spiritual exploration wrapped up in one transportable and easily accessible entertainment package.

I was brought up in a traditional early 20th Century home where the BIBLE was fed to us on a regular basis, like doses of cod liver oil. As a result, I had no appetite for it until something unexpected happened to me in Hawaii at age 30.

I was visiting Joel Goldsmith in Honolulu, and he took me over to the island of Maui to introduce me to some Kahunas and attend a lecture he was going to give. While Joel was having appointments, I borrowed a car and went up to the rim of Halealaka, the word's largest extinct volcanic crater.

No one told me that short pants and a T-shirt wouldn't do at ten thousand eight hundred feet up; so to get out of the chilling wind I got off the path and found a cave-like shelter. Sitting there meditating while waiting for the mists to clear so that I could see into the crater, I experienced something similar to hearing a recording in my head. It was on the subject of love.

Finally, to my surprise, I saw what I now consider to be the central message of the teaching we associate with the man, Jesus, yet so often hidden as if it were a secret. I have attempted to clarify the two Keys and the two stumbling blocks earlier, but it bears repeating in another way, so bear with me.

Jesus said, thou shalt Love the Lord thy God with all thy heart, and all thy Soul, and with all thy Mind. This is the first and great commandment. And the second is like unto it, Thou shalt Love thy neighbor as thy Self. On these two commandments hang all the law and the prophets.
Matthew 22:35-40

Swami Yogananada explains:

Jesus' declaration of the two greatest commandments is recounted in all three synoptic Gospels, with minor variations. The whole purpose of religion, indeed, of Life itself, is encapsulated in the two paramount commandments sighted by Lord Jesus in these verses. In them lies the essence of eternal Truth, distinguishing all bonafide spiritual paths...that man (perceiving himself) as an individualized soul separated from God must embrace...if he would reclaim the Realization of Oneness with his Maker...if you can Love God wholly in actual communion in daily meditation, and show by your actions your love for your neighbor, even as you love yourself, you will rise above the mortal consciousness of this delusive plane of life and death and realize the eternal changeless Spirit existing within yourself and in It's Everywhereness.
PARAMAHANSA YOGANANDA
THE SECOND COMING OF CHRIST
THE RESURRECTION OF THE CHRIST WITHIN YOU

Simply put, **Jesus said to love God – which in modern language means to love "Cause" – the Invisible Creative Source of life.**

And then he said for us to love our neighbors as ourselves – to love effects, which are the visible results of that which caused them to come into being.

He also added that if we could love both Cause and effect equally we would find that they are the same.

These are the complements that make the Star Keys complete. To Know God is to Love God, as to know our Oneness with Source

is to Love as Self. They have been around a long time, but have yet to become dominant in consciousness…yet.

The two complements   mean that we are not to think of ourselves as a "man" of earth or a "man" of God. Rather as the double expression of the Two Commandments, we are both. They are different dimensions of the One that I am, our job in life is to get those two "me's" to communicate with each other so that eventually they will act as One. And that this is true of everyone without exception.

The Two Commandments to love God and neighbor tell us that nothing is either/or. Sounds simple, doesn't it? Nevertheless, either/or thinking is and always has been the major cause of conflict, the mother of exclusivity, and the very thing that has kept us in material and spiritual bondage. As a whole many still define "neighbor" as separate people. Some even go so far as to believe that unless you believe in exactly the same way politically, go to the same church, and have the same ethnic background, you are not their "neighbor" and therefore are excluded from being loved.

In other words a neighbor with the possibility of being the same as self, must be a very similar human. Those that are dis-similar are not even considered a possible neighbor, rather they are excluded as an "other." Think about it and you will see that an either/or attitude still dominates politics and preempts open discussions of value. Inevitably, heated discussions dissolve into a split with one conclusion taking precedence over the other.

Either/or thinking breeds superstition.

Superstition is a belief based on fear; all fear is based on ignorance of the true Laws of the Universe.

We will discuss the Laws of the Universe in a later Chapter, but first we still have to get rid of these stumbling blocks.

GOING BEYOND SUPERSTITIONS OF FAITH

The rational for most of the world's wars has been based on a superstitious belief in God and what faith can accomplish. As long as wars and acts of terrorism are executed in the name of God, superstition rules. **We cannot solve a problem by dropping bombs or trying to force someone to act according to our cultural beliefs**. The Crusades did not stop the "infidels" from spreading their God across the Middle East and Mediterranean. The "War To End ALL Wars" did not end all wars. Our beliefs have excluded parts of the whole over and over, sometimes trying to totally eliminate the "other." Our faith has led us into battle countless times and will continue to do so until we can live beyond the superstitions of faith.

We can't sober up to reality and get rid of our religious and cultural hangovers until we become aware of how we have believed. It's surprising how many of our traditional beliefs relevant to how our good has come about and how our desires are to be fulfilled are founded on superstition. In this respect I'm sorry that we are not like computers with delete buttons that we could push and instantly send old superstitions into the trash bin.

All too often, protestations of faith are no more than endorsed superstition. No matter how often we have been told that we should have faith as though faith is a faucet that can be turned on and off – faith has most often been based on the superstitious belief that appealing to some power apart from our own Higher Consciousness can give us what we want.

At last, thanks again for our scientists who have shown us that via our perceptions, we literally affect matter; we are now able to replace superstition with fact. Saying that religious faith can now be replaced by fact sounds cold and heretical, doesn't it? It isn't. We can shout with joy, and dance in the streets because realizations that have evolved through scientific empiricism now take the guesswork out of faith. We will still have the equivalent of faith, but it won't any longer be based on superstitious projections.

Traditionally, having faith has always been centered on there being some object to have faith in. There had to be some object that one had faith in – be that a person, a teaching, a church, or a Supreme Being.

If having faith involves anything other than having an experience of one's own Higher Consciousness, it is superstition.

Consciousness is infinite.

It is superstition to believe there is anything to call upon exclusive of that which is included within one's own consciousness.

Scientists, such as Biologist Bruce Lipton, have provided us with the understanding that there is a process whereby our perceptions create our reality. The details of this process are explained in his ground breaking book, BIOLOGY OF BELIEF.

With increased awareness comes the understanding that our physical body and the objective form of our life are affected by our beliefs. Our own consciousness directly creates how our bodies function and how we personally function in life. As we move into this new cycle of evolution, we can "know" rather than superstitiously believe that some mysterious code or correctly saying our affirmations or prayers will magically fulfill our desires.

There are no accidents in consciousness; Cause and effect are one. To believe that by an act of faith we can make something happen that is not already happening is like having faith that at some future time two times two will be five. Two times two is now and always has been four. Experiencing the truth of mathematics frees one from superstition, but having faith that two times two is four won't change anything one way or the other, except perhaps, through getting the wrong answers one loses faith in one's own ability to manifest the truth.

When I say that fact replaces faith, it is because our growing capacity to "know the truth" and our scientists' ability to explain how our perceptions and mental attitudes affect our lives, eliminates the need for superstitious explanations of paranormal events such as previously unexplainable healings.

Now, we can know the unknown. We can know how and why the Spiritual Process affects us. We now know the reason that right thinking or right perceptions are causal, and being free of superstition, we can be personally in control of our lives.

Yes, we have faith – faith in our ability to know true Cause – and that faith turns belief into knowing. True Faith is Knowing.

We may not always know why specific actions necessarily produce right results, but we can remove ourselves from believing in superstitious causes by knowing that we alone are the instigators of the results we are striving for and wish to attain. It isn't as though we have faith in right thinking or right perceptions; we have faith in our ability to know how and why they operate so that we can apply them correctly and become free from superstition.

Ordinarily there is a night and day difference between "knowing" and "having faith." There is hope, faith, belief, and knowing. The first three have an element of doubt. After hope we may try to convince ourselves that we have faith and that we believe, but until the experience of knowing transcends belief it is intellectual pabulum, and for all practical purposes, sterile superstition.

It may sound shocking, but in this context we have to stop having what we have thought of as faith. **Having faith implies that one believes there is something to have faith in that is other than one's self, and some thing they do not currently possess.** Yet true faith is self-love – the recognition of self-completeness – then, faith becomes a non-existent word. It just is. We know with certainty.

In order for our beliefs to become fruitful, they must reach a certain experiential reality before they can turn into knowing. Just as water has to reach a certain temperature before it boils, **beliefs have to be experienced in consciousness where they become a living reality and transcend superstition before they become a material reality. When that happens, knowing turns into a kind of spirit/ energy that activates the knowing in a way that makes it become a self-fulfilling prophecy and not just fantasy.**

The kind of faith that is "knowing" doesn't act by committee. Committees don't create. Individuals do. Manifestation comes down to the one who knows. There is no accident or chance about it. Masters in any field do not say, "I believe." They know.

Our true home is in the present moment,
To live in the present moment is a miracle.
The miracle is not to walk on water.
The miracle is to walk on the green Earth in the present moment,
To appreciate the peace and beauty that are available now.
Peace is all around us –
In the world and in nature –
And within us –
In our bodies and our spirits.
Once we learn to touch this peace,
We will be healed and transformed,
It is not a matter of faith;
It is a matter of practice.
Thich Nhat Hanh

Mystics and Masters from east and west have told us through out this coming of age cycle, that the truth is attainable only through direct subjective experience. In Kabalistic thought, you cannot attain spiritual awareness based on beliefs, because beliefs are only our superstitions of how we think things are. One must search for themselves with clear perceptions to know spiritual truth and thus reality.

All things are too small
To hold me, I Am so vast

In the Infinite I reach
For the Uncreated
I have touched it,
It undoes me wider than wide
Everything else is too narrow
Hadewijch of Antwerp

The intellect says, "The six directions are limits: there is no way out."
Loves says, "There is a way: I have traveled it thousands times." Rumi

It is up to the individual. No one can fulfill another's expectations for them yet each of us, through an act of free will, can become alive in our expectations consciously activated through realization, through knowing. When that happens we experience a higher dimension of our being freed of limitations – at which time "YE ARE GODS."

BEYOND GOOD & EVIL

I hope we are clarifying the process as we move forward. But there are still more stumbling blocks along the way, such as doing away with good and evil.

Can you image a world where good and evil does not exist? Oh you say "Great! Eliminate evil, and then all we have is good." But this will not be so. Like-wise those who say God is only Love are excluding the full spectrum of God.

Good is not exclusive of evil and likewise they are both dimensions of the energy of one Creative Source.

By our not having understood the purpose and meaning of good and evil, we have accepted a false belief in duality and given birth to anxiety and depression.

To explain, as long as we believe that good and evil are in opposition to each other, we create a false division of the One Energy of life. Indeed, we all have moments when we are uncomfortable and ill at ease because of some major or minor obstruction, and at other times we feel free and unobstructed, but what we haven't accepted is that each is necessary for progress. When we understand the creative nature of life, we become aware that moving forward requires being both in balance and out of balance. That's the *modus operandi* for walking.

Balance is a process of moving in and out, it is the flow of life.

When times are rough we do not have to insult our intelligence by denying our uncomfortable and sometimes painful feelings, fearing that if we acknowledge them we are contradicting our belief that God is the only power.

As long as we know that despite appearances there is a Divine Process at work that will ultimately give birth to our fulfillment, we transcend the belief that good is opposed to evil or that there is a power other than Omnipotence.

Religions contradict the supposition that God is the only power by implying that our goal should be to overcome all discomfort or difficulty through faith. This can be in the faith that God will save them from problems and pain, or that your faith sees all suffering as an illusion.

We have no problems – we have opportunities for which we should give thanks. Edgar Cayce

The truth is that our finest moments are most likely to occur – when we are feeling deeply uncomfortable, unhappy, or unfulfilled. For it is only in such moments, propelled by our discomfort, that we are likely to step out of our ruts and start searching for different ways or truer answers. M. Scott Peck

Our growing spiritual awareness tells us that all creativity involves what is only seemingly a problem, but in reality is an opportunity. When one does not resist the Process, the difficult times are transmuted more readily with positive and creative results. When we hold on to judgment of good and evil, we limit the flow of the creative process to move through infinite plays of energy as life seeks Divine expression through Love and Harmony. Resistance binds us to immobility.

It is, indeed, a matter of life or death. **Life is movement and movement requires being in and out of balance. Life is not always balanced, that would be stagnation.**

A tightrope walker is a good example. The only way he or she can make it across the rope is to lean to one side and then to the other in order to average a kind of balance that could not otherwise be attained. To seek security is to seek stagnation and death.

To be grateful for the difficult as well as the easy is to welcome life.

The difference between judging, or seeing good and evil as being in opposition to each other is resolved by realizing that they are two sides of one coin. Our judgments, whether good or bad, are based on a belief in two powers and are therefore illusions. There is but One. Mystics who claim that there is no evil power are telling us the truth when we understand that what we call evil is not really evil because it is part of growth and evolution.

To move forward as living mystics we will experience living beyond the limitations of good and evil. Judgments then become merely viewpoints within the on going Divine Process.

BEYOND HOPE

Why would we want to go beyond hope? Don't we want to hope that things turn out well? The real question is: What do we want to create?

Hope binds one's thoughts to a state of creativeness that is uncertain; whereas knowing projects one's intention into manifestation with positive energy. Knowing one's true Being or Godliness is a belief in the certainty of an outcome. This is true knowing.

Creating with hope allows for other possibilities, because one is creating with less than a certainty of one's true Oneness with Source.

Creating with the positive knowingness of ones true identity empowers and propels us beyond hope.

Hope implies a lack of trusting the Process, a lack of Knowing. Hope actually re-enforces human fear. Hope is not a statement of trust or knowing. Currently we stand in one dimension, "hoping" we will enter into the new era of God Consciousness, as multi-dimensional beings. We will enter, because we are already on the journey and we know we are guided by an invisible hand, The Divine Process.

"Going Beyond" means, to totally let go of something we have held on to in the past. As we move into greater levels of living our Higher Consciousness, we no longer hope that our Divinity guides our lives, we know with certainty that we are that Divinity.

The positive action of letting go of old paradigms allows us to be aware that the Divine activity of Grace flows as our life Process. Grace goes before us to make the crooked places straight.

Grace is the positive flow of high vibrational energy returning to us when we send out our own ripples of God Consciousness. Thus Grace is the wave of the Universe (God) responding to itself in a heightened vibrational state.

We are now being called to live fully with the knowledge that our consciousness is moving us from a waffling position between dimensions to a stand up position of such a complete acceptance of our Divinity that we act with confidence and conviction.

To fully experience the livingness of our Divine Humanity, we have to completely give up the ways of thinking that create a lack of belief in all that we are. Hope allows for other possibilities to manifest that may be far less than what one intends.

It's time we create with conviction. It's time we create from the knowingness of our Higher Consciousness directly infusing the unlimited power of the Universe into any situation.

As our dear friend and fellow spirit on the path, Ernie Fitzpatrick (leader of the Life Revealing Community) has expressed, "The

Universe is recording our every move." The wholeness of the Universe listens to every word and thought you have and responds accordingly. And what do you think it does when it hears you say, "I hope this happens?" The Universal All-ness responds with uncertainty just as you project it out there. It cannot do anything else. Every thought that comes into your creative Process is recorded in the media field of the creative Universe.

Compile a lot of wishful thinking, a stack of hopeful prayers, with a few positive affirmations for good measure, and the outcome is a jumble of intentions in a field of uncertainty. However when we stand up with fervor, abandon all hope, and totally create with the positive conviction of our Divine Self, the outcome travels along lines of positive manifestation. The dictionary defines fervor with a list of positive words that show the power of ardent conviction. Creating with fervor infuses our creative Process with spiritual fire, with divine energy directly from Source.

So if the Universe is recording your every action, wouldn't you want your Divine passion, your zeal for living the fullness of your Christ awareness to arise and shine to the full measure of your unbound Divinity? Absolutely!

So stand up with me and live with passionate fervor, abandon all hope, and choose your highest potential in every Grace filled opportunity. This is living as the Gods of the New Age.

THE CAUSE AND EFFECT SUPERSTITION

When the so called metaphysical movement began to make an impact on America at the beginning of the 20th Century and when Christian Science churches began to appear in most cities, Quantum Physicists had not yet proposed their concept that consciousness was the creative, maintaining, and sustaining reality of material effects. Nevertheless, the Christian Scientists based their teaching on the belief that there was no cause in effects, that Spirit or "Divine Principle" was the only Cause.

The central belief of Christian Science is found in a short paragraph, which begins:

> *There is no life, truth, intelligence, nor substance in matter. All is Infinite Mind and its infinite manifestation, for God is All-in-all. Spirit is immortal Truth; matter is mortal error. Spirit is the real and eternal; matter is the unreal and temporal. Spirit is God, and man is His image and likeness. Therefore man is not material; he is spiritual.*
> Mary Baker Eddy, SCIENCE AND HEALTH

This metaphysical truth reverses Cause and effect by realizing that matter is not the cause, it is only an effect. If generally accepted, the concept that effects are not cause would put Madison Avenue advertising agencies out of business. Every TV commercial sets out to convince the public that its product can cause something desirable to happen. It's the same with the pharmaceutical suppliers who try to convince the public that their health depends on the advertised drug. It does unless superstition is replaced by a true understanding of the relationship of cause and effect.

There is no cause in an effect. The drug is an effect. **Your own subjective consciousness places cause where you will.**

Your consciousness as Cause, creates health, wealth, sickness, or lack.

If the Quantum Physicists are correct, no one has ever been killed by a bullet. If we put a bullet, an effect, on a table and wait for it to kill someone, we'd have a long wait. Someone had to consciously make the bullet, had to consciously put it in a gun, had to consciously aim the gun and pull the trigger. The consciousness of those who manufactured the guns and bullets and of the one who pulled the trigger killed the person, not the bullet. There is no intelligence in a bullet. It can't do anything of itself. An atomic bomb cannot drop itself. An act of terrorism cannot come about of itself. It takes consciousness to make these things happen.

In other words, consciousness, not an effect, is Cause, and it is a form of superstition to believe that effects are Cause.

That does not exclude using effects, such as pharmaceuticals. They are the result of consciousness as well. **Knowing that consciousness or spirit is Cause eliminates superstition, and instead of being used by effects one can use them and depend on the power of consciousness as Cause.**

Then if results are not attainable through certain effects, consciousness will take care of it or lead to other effects that reflect the needed consciousness.

My understanding of what I just said was a long time coming. My father, grandfather, and uncle were all medical doctors. They were quite vocal about their belief that something should be done about Christian Scientists who through their "miss-understood faith" allowed their children to suffer rather than turning to medical science for help. Those "misguided" Christian Science parents were right in having discovered that spirit or consciousness was the ultimate power and that it could produce spontaneous healings, but because they did not double-think, they turned a half-truth into superstition. If they had understood that what medical science had to offer was a byproduct of spirit as well, their children might not have suffered.

I finally came to understand that it's not a matter of whether we use effects or not, but rather of our dependency on them. Spontaneous healings without medical intervention do take place at times, and of course medical science also saves lives. All the wonderful things that science, man's creative ingenuity, and spiritual consciousness produces are here for our use and enjoyment.

We can use these effects and not be used by them if we are dependent on the consciousness that the effects symbolize and not on the effects themselves.

I take vitamins, use medications on occasion, and drink a glass of wine when I feel like it, but if I were to find myself being dependent on any of these things I would re-examine my thinking. If I was enslaved by the belief that I had to follow a rigid timetable for when, where, or how much to imbibe, it would be a sign of my being dependent.

To be dependent on any created thing is another form of superstition. My dependency is on the consciousness that has created the effects I use, not on the effects themselves.

If I eat fatty foods and think that is going to make me fat and eventually kill me, I might in fact get fat and die of clogged arteries; but the fatty foods did not do it, my over–all consciousness manifested as my own behavior.

My first priority has to be to have the consciousness of health, of vitality, of life everlasting. We have to be fearless enough to look behind our superstitious beliefs to find the casual consciousness.

Superstition

Let's look at the ways that in the name of Divinity we have perpetuated superstition. It is superstitious to believe that good can come to us as though some outside source bestowed it upon us. All good already exists. It can only come from us – from our realized consciousness of it.

The belief that the things we want are drawn to us by anything other than our own consciousness is superstition.

Fear is superstition at its worst.

When a government, church, or organization fosters fear, they tempt us to make that superstitious fear into a self-fulfilling prophecy, and those individuals who buy into it pay the price.

To believe that there is a supreme being that is in one place and not another, or in one person and not another, is superstition.

To believe that others are somehow obligated to take care of our needs is a form of superstition.

For that matter, to believe that our good comes from another person suggests that an object, a person, is Cause, and that is a superstition.

Your good may come via another person, but if that good were not already in your consciousness it would not have become your self-realization.

On the other hand, when you appreciate how the Spirit enhances your life through, or as another person, that is how and why you love that person.

Our own Higher Consciousness is life, and life is self-sustained. To pray for life to be more alive is superstition. **To believe that our health, our weather, our good fortune, our companionship, or our new opportunities come from something outside of our own consciousness is superstition.** All those things can and do come into manifestation by a Divine Process that is taking place in and as us. They come from our experiencing our own Divine Consciousness. To believe they come from a Cause outside of ourselves is superstition at its most delusional.

We become free when we consciously realize that there isn't anything or anyone outside of our own selves that can keep us from self-fulfilling knowledge. Then we become aware that we can turn on our protective, creative, and rewarding spiritual energy at any time. It not only frees us from the tyranny of undiscovered truths that we may not have been fortunate enough to have come across, but it lifts us into **the realization that we are "now" all that we have thought Divinity to be**.

We may not be able to make it work on cue, but our potential is limitless and it is superstition to look to anyone or anything outside of our own selves for the fulfillment of our needs. That is not to say that our fulfillment might not come in the form of a person, place, or thing, but all are a part of our own consciousness manifesting in form. There is no thing separate. Only what is in our own consciousness manifests in our life.

When I say that the answers are all within our own selves, I don't want for one second to take the sense of magic out of life. The fact that the answer to all of our desires is in and as our own consciousness is just as awe inspiring and amazing as anything can be. It literally opens our potential to infinite possibilities. **Our ability to make conscious contact with our own Divine Consciousness is the miracle of miracles.**

When Jesus said, "your faith hath made you whole," he was trying to counter superstition by explaining that he himself, apart from representing the potential in all of us, hadn't done anything miraculous. The person's own perception and consciousness had done it.

The word consciousness did not exist 2,000 years ago, but I am sure it would have been used if Jesus were teaching today. **Jesus voiced the truth that one's own conscious realization becomes that person's self-fulfilling prophecy. In other words – we don't have to look outside of our own selves for our good.**

Jesus also said, "Whatever ye ask for, believing ye shall receive." **He was saying that if one's belief reaches the experiential level of the energy of knowing, it becomes a self-fulfilling prophecy for that one, and that which one perceives automatically comes about.**

"I hope," "I believe," and "I have faith" all endorse superstition, but "I know," says "It is," and whatever is envisioned becomes fact.

What I am beholding is significant in the evolutionary process of expanding consciousness even though it flies in the face of accepted popular theology. That means that I must be careful not to load too much on to unprepared thought.

In other words, the language I use that is designed to eliminate old superstitions and dualistic thinking needs careful explanation or it will seem to contradict the very foundation of faith. If I am successful, faith will be revitalized and reinforced by being freed from dogma and misinterpretation rather than it being eliminated.

As a result, I feel that the next few years will lead us all, knowingly or unknowingly, into the new cycle of life based on a new level of awareness that will be strong enough to create changes within the consciousness of the whole. There is no accident that Eron and I are writing this material to help lead the way or that you are reading it. We all have a part to play in the evolution of consciousness into this New Age.

I know this whole truth is a huge stumbling block. It flies in the face of our conditioned reality, our eons-old beliefs, and "normal" human perception. And you can't get beyond our old concepts without the Keys and their double nature. Even a mystical experience or an encounter with Jesus himself, might not break the bonds of old conditioning. But over time, which is what we do have in this dimension, consciousness evolves. Trust the Process and allow Grace to move through you.

Once we pass through our limiting concepts we realize the Universe is an infinity of vibrational pathways of creativity. Posed in the middle of the Milky Way on the beginning of this new 26,000 year cycle, we can open countless magical doors with the Star Keys of the Universe. So let's continue to let go of outmoded concepts.

Superstition of God

Most significantly, before we can even begin to attain the deeper levels of the mystical experience to which our spiritual evolution has brought us to today, there is one all important major stumbling block we have to deal with – the superstition of God!

If it sounds sacrilegious to say we have to get rid of God, I mean for it to. Before we can fully love ourselves and experience who we are in the here and now, we have to let go of the divisive concepts of God that are associated with the word and its equivalent in the world's religions, such as Allah, or Brahman. Not only has God been an excuse to kill countless people, but nothing has universally kept individuals from knowing who they are and the freedoms that they are capable of enjoying than what we think of as God.

We have been taught all our lives to believe that God is a Supreme Being, a concept, something outside of and apart from ourselves; so no matter how hard we try, it is almost impossible for any of us, me included, to think of or use the word without somehow still feeling that God is something other than our own Being. We may have taken the first step by believing that God is "in" us, but that still implies God "and" us, some thing in some thing else. As it is impossible for us to eliminate the word from our vocabulary, we have no choice but to reinterpret it or we will remain victims of our religions.

Religions, by and large, are primarily man-made philosophies, parables, and superstitions that have kept humankind in bondage to a concept of our becoming something in the "future", rather than something we are "now." Religions tell us that God will affect our lives if, when, and after we conform to the rules. Adding fuel to the fire, religions lie to us by telling us that until we adhere to God's wishes, God is not present in our lives.

Fortunately, the God religions refer to does not exist.

Unfortunately, we can't avoid using the word altogether or it would just fester in our unconscious and subconsciously poison us.

So what can we do about it? We have no choice but to deal with it, perhaps appreciate the intent behind how it is used even when there is a fraudulent application of the word, and replace it with the truth.

If we are going to continue using the word, "God" at all, for all practical purposes we can begin by understanding that there are basically two concepts of God, a lie and a truth.

The truth is that God is the subjective and impersonal expression of prime Cause or existence, which is beyond words and thoughts, though possible for us to experience. That's the truth.

The lie is an objective, mental, or a personal concept of the existence of an entity called God, something other than and exclusive of humankind.

John quotes Jesus as saying "God is Spirit, and they that worship him must worship in spirit and in truth." "It is the Spirit that gives life; the flesh is no help at all." John 4:24 & 6:63 – which is pretty clear, and probably the word closest to "consciousness" at that time.

However, we can't reprint the BIBLE and all the books of the past; so the best we can do is to instantly disenfranchise the word, and automatically reinterpret it with a new meaning, one that is consistent with the *Double Thread* truth of our Being, which is both human and Divine.

We have to watch out, however, and not resist what intention people have behind what they mistakenly think of as God. Everyone is reaching out to his or her highest sense of the meaning of life. "Resist not evil" applies to our feelings toward how others use the word God, as well.

Whatever ignorance you resist you perpetuate, because resistance gives it substance. What we resist we create. No, if we want to get rid of the onus of a mistaken concept of a God that is other than our own being, we have to replace it rather than resist it.

When we see or hear the word, God, we have to get to the point where in our thinking minds we automatically and instantly replace the lie with a truth. Indeed there is but One Cause, One Creation, and One Divine Process. Indeed, whatever that is, it is not a Supreme Being sitting on a supernatural cloud. It's not an "it." It's a Presence. Let's call it the Presence of Truth, Supreme Knowledge, Divine or Higher Consciousness. As such it is ever–present everywhere and it is the substance that makes up all things whether we recognize it or not. That means it is present right where we are individually.

As it is not a thing, God must be an experience of consciousness, Divine Consciousness. That is what we must automatically

remember every time we hear the word.

Boiled down to two words: **God is Divine Consciousness.**

This is what I do: Every time I see or hear the word, God, I automatically and instantly think "my own Higher Consciousness," or "Divine Consciousness." When that truth is instantly affirmed duality ceases to exist and Omnipresence remains a livable fact to me, both visibly and invisibly.

You may ask, "Then how do I consciously access or experience this Divine Consciousness that is my true being when I need to?" In the old days when we believed in a supreme being, we prayed to it. Presently we can do the same; however, now, in what we might call our prayers, we are appealing to and reaching out to our own Higher Consciousness – nothing apart from ourselves. We can literally talk to and pray to our own Divine Consciousness. Perhaps that is what Jesus meant when he said the Kingdom was within, or as our own consciousness. What else is closer than hands and feet?

Our consciousness has it's home in Kingdom Consciousness,

If we consciously open ourselves to our Higher Consciousness miracles may seem to happen, because our Higher Consciousness knows our intent, and intent manifests in our outer lives. If we seek guidance, we will mentally hear the answer we seek coming from the infinity that is our Higher Consciousness.

When we can see the difference between ordinary imagination and our intuition, we become aware that our intuition is how our Divine Consciousness speaks to us. Meditation is then not a spiritual matter so much as an attempt to listen to our Higher Consciousness, our intent to open ourselves to Universal Truth – not someone else's, some other entity's, or a church's truth – but the Truth that is included in and as our own being, the Truth that is Universal, Infinite and All-Inclusive.

GOD IS NOTHING

Once more trying to de-condition our old concept of God, we'll tackle it from another angle. God is nothing. **God, as a mentally created concept, is nothing. If God were some thing it would be limited.** To believe in God is to believe in something, and if God is beyond words and thoughts, what is there to believe in? You either experience it or you don't.

To do away with believing in a superstitious God, there is something Divine that we can experience. Experience is different than believing. You become an experience, but you have to have something or some concept to believe in, in order to believe.

Why do we fear to not believe in a God? We fear letting go of limitation. **We fear being responsible for our lives. We fear being free, and as long as we believe in and give power to a concept of God, we are not free.** We are taught that we should feel love for God, and that leads us up the garden path. In order to love there has to be some "thing" to love, and again, **God is not a thing.**

In the same way, trying to love God is to pursue the impossible, because the finite cannot embrace the infinite. **The closest we can come to loving God is to love ourselves - and life's other creations.**

To love all as all, is hard to do with our present grip on old concepts. To Love God is to Know the Truth of the First Star Key. **Then as Global Spiritualized Beings, we will be able Love as God and ourselves, inclusively. Then to Love God is to Love as God.**

The closest we can come while still at the level of words and thoughts is to love IS-ness.

Just know all is, and do not define what it is.

God Is, and yet, God is nothing.

God is both the seen and unseen, as we are both the seen and unseen.

We are made in the image of God. That means we and our loved ones have to stop believing in or loving appearances as though they are an end in themselves.

What most people call love is no more than a concept of their own desires fulfilled, perhaps in or as another person but it is their own thought-consent they are responding to. To truly love a person is to simultaneously realize that they are not made in the image of an imagined God but, rather, that they exist in the flesh as Divine Beings beyond words and thoughts.

Hear these words and you may easily think, "They have taken away my Lord." Indeed, if getting rid of the old superstitious concept of God means we have taken away your God, I hope we have. We have to if we want to proclaim the Gospel truth. **The good news is that experiencing your own inner Divine Being will bring into your lives all that you turned to God for in the past.**

It is the only way to achieve what we turned to religion for in the past. In the past answered prayer was hit or miss; not now. That is why we say that this realization of God as one's own Higher Consciousness gives faith back to us in the way it should be. This is being a Globalized Spiritual Being.

If you are still stumbling on this Truth that God is your own Higher Consciousness, perhaps it is because you are seeing your Higher Consciousness as limited.

Your Higher Consciousness is infinite, endlessly intertwined with All That Is, As ALL THAT IS, Omnipotence, Omniscience, and Omnipresence.

We are not saying that your personal consciousness or even your vast subconscious mind is your Higher Consciousness. You are not limited by your personal physical, mental, and emotional systems.

When there is no limiting "thing" to hang on to, not even a concept of God, God is no longer a superstition, and one is finally free to love and experience who they are.

You are not a "thing." You are Consciousness appearing visibly, and as Consciousness, embrace all things, nothing exclusively.

In this New Age, we can experience our own Divine Being, this is realizing our Divinity as Global Spiritual Beings – Cosmic Infinite Beings!

Meditation

The number one deceit designed by ignorance is to separate us from God. The second is a mistaken advocacy of meditation or prayer. If belief in God as separate from our own being is the number one deceit, the belief that we can attain our freedom in the future through meditation or prayer is the second.

The word "meditation" and the word "mediation" are almost identical. **To mediate between the human and the Divine is to close the gap between our personal sense of self and our spiritual reality as the Presence of the Divine Now.**

Therefore, any belief that you can get some "thing" from praying, or that you can call on God, or your own Higher Consciousness to make something happen, does exactly the opposite of what you have intended. Instead, you actually affirm lack, and place yourself under a law of limitation that makes what you desire almost impossible to manifest. It causes you to think you are separate from your good, and your meditation doesn't become mediation between your personal sense of self and the Divine you.

The minute you seek something in meditation you affirm that you don't have it. That even includes your desire to feel the Presence of the Divine.

If you go to meditation without seeking to experience something that you hope to become but rather for meditation to be a way for you to recognize that you already are Divine, then your meditation does not have a purpose based on something that does not already exist.

Perhaps surprisingly, **when you don't try to make it happen in the future it appears in the present**. It does. In other words, let your meditation be based on "I have," and you will.

That is why Goldsmith and others say that our goal is to go beyond words and thoughts, all words and thoughts, even those about spiritual matters, particularly those involving a concept of God. The paradox is that if you put into your intent the desire to transcend a sense of duality and then let it go, you will find yourself beyond the thoughts that have kept you in bondage.

Allow the mystical to be experienced.

Allow meditation to Be, Just Be.

Don't use meditation. Be used by it. To meditate for the love of it is to let meditation use you for the glory of your Self.

MEISTER ECKHART

After writing about God, we decided to once more look into the teaching of Meister Eckhart, that 14th Century mystic who was excommunicated by the Inquisition. Once more we were fascinated at his agreement with what we have been experiencing and to the additions I feel we can now add to his revelation. A prerequisite of evolution is that the minute something new evolves, the past is obsolete, not valueless but obsolete. As consciousness evolves, new understandings clear what was hard to express as it first emerged.

Eckhart was a master at exposing false religious concepts but still wasn't able to take the *Double Thread* step of seeing the human as an expression of the Divine. Most of Eckhart's writings deal with the creature/self and are telling him or her how to deny themselves. In one of his last sermons, however, he came as close to the real truth as was possible then, and ended it by saying that most people would not understand what he was saying – and they haven't, because few can even see it today.

Here are a few passages of the sermon that got him excommunicated. In order to clarify confusion, we have taken the liberty of putting God in lower case when Eckhart is talking of a personalized God and upper case when he is referring to the mystical God.

> *Back in the womb from which I came, I had no god and merely was myself. I did not will or desire anything, for I was pure being, a knower of myself by Divine Truth. Then I wanted myself and thus I existed untrammeled by god or anything else...*

> *Now we say that a god, in so far that he is only god, is not the highest goal of creation nor is his fullness of being as great as that of the least of creatures, themselves in God. Therefore we pray that we may be rid of god, and taking the truth, break into eternity, where the highest souls are too, are like what I was in my primal existence, when I wanted what I was and was what I wanted.*

> *The authorities say that God is a being, an intelligent being who knows everything, But I say that God is neither a being nor intelligent and he does not "know" either this or that. God is free of everything and therefore he is everything.*

> *I pray God that he may quit me of god, for unconditional being is above god and all distinctions. It was here that I was myself, wanted myself, and knew myself to be this person (here before you) and therefore, I Am my own first Cause, both of my eternal being and of my temporal being.*

> *To this end I was born, and by virtue of my birth being eternal, I shall never die. It is of the nature of this eternal birth that I have been eternally, that I Am now, and shall be forever. What I am as a temporal creature is to die and come to nothingness.*

> *For it came with time and so with time it will pass away. In my eternal birth, however, everything was begotten. I was my own first Cause as well as the first Cause of everything else. If I had not been, there would have been no God.*

There is, however, no need to understand this.
Meister Eckhart

If what Eckhart or we have said is too much to wrap your mind around, great! Perhaps that is its virtue. We are never closer than when we no longer try to understand and just surrender to the truth of our own being.

Know that going beyond your concept of God, your belief in faith, your view of meditation, and hope are all huge stumbling blocks that fly in the face of our conditioned reality, our eons-old beliefs, and "normal" human perception. And you can't get there without the Keys and their double nature. Even a mystical experience or an encounter with Jesus himself, might not break the bonds of old conditioning. But over time, which is what we do have in this dimension, consciousness evolves.

> *Although you can not know consciousness, you can become conscious of it as yourself. You sense it directly in any situation, no matter where you are. You can sense it here and now as your very Presence, the inner space in which the words on this page are perceived and become thoughts. It is the underlying I AM.*
> Eckhart Tolle, **A New Earth**

Trust the Process and allow Grace to move through you.

We are not going to leave you out on a limb, now we'll proceed to exploring how these Keys work in the Divine Process. First we have to clarify what we mean by Divine Process.

Chapter Three

Trust the Process

THE DIVINE PROCESS

OK, let's try on the new concept that everything we see is consciousness manifesting in form and put an end to the old superstitious belief that there is a God outside of ourselves determining the way our lives unfold. In doing so, let's look at how consciousness works in our lives. During the last few decades of this revolutionary cycle, Quantum Physicists such as John S. Belle and John Clasuser made what has been called by physicist Henry Stapp the most important discovery in the history of Science. They took science beyond rational thought.

Stapp states, "If the statistical predictions of quantum theory are true, an objective universe is incompatible with the law of local causes." He means that the objective universe does not exist apart from consciousness.

> *No objective phenomenon exists with an independent or intrinsic identity...The notion of a pre-given, observer-independent reality is untenable. As in the new physics, matter cannot be objectively perceived or described apart from the observer.*
> Dalai Lama, THE UNIVERSE IN A SINGLE ATOM

In Vedantic vernacular, this verified what the teachings have postulated – that is that the world is a dream of consciousness. In fact, they did more than that. They realized that even a tiny electron is connected to every other electron in the universe.

The Dalai Lama also writes that a Mahayana text, THE FLOWER ORNAMENT SCRIPTURE, "*in beautiful poetic verse, compares the intricate and profoundly interconnected reality of the world to an infinite net of gems called Indra's jeweled Net, which reaches out to infinite space. At each knot on the net is crystal gem, which is connected to all the other gems and reflects it's self in all the others.*"

Likewise, Belle and Clasuser's Quantum theorem states that objects such as electrons even though separated and placed at the furthest distances of the universe, would still be in in-separable contact. Furthermore, they are constantly in touch through consciousness, not form, with all that is. They implied that if we think of God as being the Creator Consciousness, then our own consciousness is God because it created us.

As nothing at the level of thought is complete without its compliment, we have to ask ourselves what is needed to make that knowledge effective? To be effective it needs an appreciation of the Process of expanding consciousness through multi-dimensions; the Process is needed to translate thought into form.

The Process is creation in action.

The Process is the turning Key that allows the vibrations of Infinite Source to flow in and through and as our lives.

The Process is God creating.

In other words, trying on the new concept does nothing unless we apply it to our lives. Again this is the First Star Key revealing the Second, then using the Keys to open new pathways of consciousness out-picturing as our lives; thus we evolve forward into greater expressions of Love, Light, Joy, and Harmony.

God is Consciousness. Activating this Consciousness is the Divine Process at work in our lives as our individual lives.

Whether he knew it or not, when the author of the GOSPEL OF JOHN opened it by saying that *"In the beginning is the Word and the Word is made flesh"* he was not only saying that consciousness becomes form, he was also announcing a priority.

In the beginning the Process is subjective, which through the process of imagination (image-initiation) then becomes form. Of course, the author of JOHN was talking about Jesus; so the Word he was referring to was positive and creative; whereas, in everyday life the Word can also be destructive as well as creative, which means that how we appreciate and see the Process is all important.

We are the Process, so it is important how we create our individual flow.

The Process is actually impersonal. It is a function of Creative Source, and it is working whether you trust it or not.

With our expanding awareness we have choices, albeit only in time and space. **We are the directors of our consciousness and thus how the Process manifests as the flow of our life.** The extreme disorder that characterizes the current flow characterizes the shift of expanding consciousness, when and how is up to us in our earthly space-time.

"A rose by any other name," applies to all the world's religious concepts of a Divine Process. **To truly place one's faith in this Omnipotent power one has to transcend the belief in good and evil as two powers.**

For that to happen one has to replace a fundamentally objective viewpoint, which is the visible approach, with trust in the invisible subjective nature of life.

For those who do, it means they primarily live in, or are motivated by an invisible world. This is the Key to Spiritual evolution.

When I say, "primarily live in an invisible world," I do so because those who have attempted to live only in an invisible world, claiming that the visible is illusion, have ended up with the most miserable of lives fraught with poverty and pain. Unfortunately, that has included a great portion of society, mainly in the Orient, where the Christ teaching of the Word made flesh is not seen as the invisible creating the visible.

As a matter of fact, I feel a depth of gratitude for Emerson and Mary Baker Eddy. They borrowed the illusory nature of life from the Orient and combined it with the Western message that includes the Word made flesh.

Lulled by stupefying illusions,
the world is asleep in the cradle of infancy,
dreaming away the hours.
Material sense does not unfold the facts of existence;
but spiritual sense lifts human consciousness into
eternal Truth.
Mary Baker Eddy

All our progress is an unfolding, like a vegetable bud. You have first an instinct, then an opinion, then a knowledge as the plant has root, bud, and fruit. Trust the instinct to the end, though you can render no reason.
Ralph Waldo Emerson

Teilhard de Chardin's prayer opened the door further:

"Lay hold on me fully both by the without and the within.
May I never break this double thread."

Obviously, that impressed me so greatly that I borrowed the words, "the double thread" for the title of my first book.

In a round about way, I am trying to show that there is a Divine Process at work in all creation. The stages that a concept goes through from its inception to the resultant visible form is due to this creative Process.

If the process is harmonious the results are harmonious.

If the consciousness of the individual process is confused the results reflect the confusion.

However the larger all-inclusive Divine Process is always expanding toward greater Harmony and Love.

As we have said, in the evolutionary process effecting an individual's spiritual consciousness there comes a time when a shift begins to take place lifting that person from their having a primarily objective or visible approach to life, into the primacy and awareness of an invisible or Spiritual Process at work.

There is another step, the realization that they are themselves the Divine Process that they have been seeking to find.

In order to prepare them for the next step, mystics, almost as a necessary cleansing, often experience what is commonly known of as "a dark night of the soul." As a result of this purging, the seeker comes to realize that he or she is not only affected by the Process, but that they are also the Process itself. They are the Process and their physical body is the visible result. The answer then becomes obvious. **If we are the Process and are unhappy with the results that have appeared in our lives, through our spiritual consciousness we can change them.**

In my own life, freedom came alive for me when I began to realize that I am not only this Process, but that it is also the same Process that makes the flowers bloom in the spring, that makes the world go round and, above all, is the Process that fills my heart with love, not just localized love but Universal Love. Through Universal Love I saw that though I have thought there was such a thing as space, that is an illusion.

The air I live in and through is filled with substances that my eyes do not see and is the same air that you live in; we are all connected to each other in this field. It is not an empty field; it is full of consciousness. That consciousness connects us all.

There is only One and all of us are that One. That is the Process of Universal Love. And to love it is to trust it. It's that simple.

HONESTY

Honestly, you are the Process that creates your life. Be honest with yourself and you will enjoy yourself. Self-honesty is not a matter of refusing to tell a lie. It is a matter of trusting yourself as being the Divine Process. When Shakespeare said, "To thine own self be true," he was advising us to be honest with ourselves. Yes, being honest may seem momentarily disruptive to old patterns, but if we trust the Process in the end our self-confidence will prove the efficacy of our trust in remarkable ways.

Without self-love it is impossible to be honest.

Some times it is being spiritually honest to tell a little white lie. White lies are those, which are made in love at those times when the truth would be harmful if not hateful. It is a matter of replacing hurtful words with more tactful or even uplifting words. That's why I say there are two kinds of honesty. One is based on a literal interpretation of spoken words, and the other on the truthfulness inherent in the consciousness of the Process or Spirit that is present, though perhaps hidden in the words.

Love will always lead you toward harmony.

You can feel harmony within your own vibrations; you can trust your feelings to reflect these vibrations.

Honesty is compassion beyond personal perceptions of right and wrong.

If you want others to be happy, practice compassion.

If you want to be happy, practice compassion.

Before we can generate compassion and love, it is important to have a clear understanding of what we understand compassion and love to be. **In simple terms, compassion and love can be defined as positive thoughts and feelings that give rise to such essential things in life as hope, courage, determination, and inner strength.**

In the Buddhist tradition, compassion and love are seen as two aspects of the same thing: Compassion is the wish for another being to be free from suffering; love is wanting them to have happiness.

His Holiness the Dalai Lama, THE COMPASSIONATE LIFE

Today there is epidemic of "bullying" that is based on personal judgments of right and wrong or good and bad. Bullies are often "honest" to a fault in that they only see their view that is blindly stated without regard for the well being of the person being bullied. This is the blindness of honesty.

Without the love of Self that sees the Oneness of each individual within the whole, there is no compassionate honesty. The truth in the paradox here is that the bully also lacks Self-Love and the realization that they too are One with all.

Honesty is the kindness of Self lifting Self.

The Divine Process sees all with the eyes of compassion.

YOU CAN TRUST THE PROCESS

To Trust the Process is to live by Grace. Grace isn't an idea. It is energy. When the Scriptures say that Grace came by Jesus the Christ it is talking about a new dispensation that Jesus introduced, a new way of living called the Christ Spirit. The Old Testament way is to live by laws based on the belief in two powers, bad and good, rather than the belief that there is but One Power and One Presence, a Divine Process.

To live by Grace is to live by intuition, Spirit and, most importantly, trusting in the Process.

Let me clarify here that when I say "Jesus," I am referring to the individual Presence of God Consciousness, or Christ Consciousness, that taught as Jesus.

Jesus introduced the belief that Love was our sufficiency in all things. That means that when we trust the Process we are trusting Grace as the energy of Love. Trusting the Process is a form of surrender. **Surrender is not a passive act. It takes strength and fortitude to surrender. In fact, it takes a complete trust in one's Self, which is Self-Love.**

Surrendering to the Process is an internal matter, as one surrenders one's self to ones own higher Conscious-Self. In fact, when one surrenders the belief that one has any needs that can only be filled from something outside of ones self, they are acknowledging that they already have all they need. That is why surrendering to the Process is not defeat but success, not an act of accepting insufficiency but of recognizing abundance.

Perhaps, part of us always feels that there is some power outside of ourselves. That is all right. When one is feeling finite there is something outside of that attitude to surrender to. As Infinite Beings we are capable of experiencing every emotion. It is all right as long as we remember that it is our nature to be infinite. This can be a stumbling block unless you can think of yourself as infinite, existing on many levels, no matter what temporary circumstance you might find yourself. The human-body, you is not all of you. It might not be able to see beyond its temporary limitations, but you can trust that your Infinite Consciousness does.

To Trust the Process is to surrender the belief that there is any power apart from one's own Self.

To surrender to the Process is to accept the fact that one Is the Process, that the Process is their being, not something outside of one's self but inside as well.

To live by Grace is to Trust the Process. Grace is the energy of Spirit, the Holy Spirit.

Surrender is my peace I give you, not as the world give I, but my peace.

DECEPTIVE GRACE

Yes, Grace can be deceptive if we do not encompass the whole of its truth. I remember when, after years of hearing about a life lived by Grace, of trying to turn my life over to Grace, and of Trusting the Process known as Grace, in my later years I finally surrendered to what I thought was getting myself out of the way and living by Grace.

As I mentioned when I resigned from the Unity board and cleared my deck, I had no future lecture commitments and was now going to live purely by Grace. That meant that if I needed companionship, needed someone to help me drive the car and such that Grace would provide. I sat there dead in the water, so to speak. Despite the fact that I daily reaffirmed my desire to let Grace direct my activities and my life, nothing happened. I was at peace but it was a kind of escapist peace based on letting go of outer activity. Companionship didn't walk through the door. Lecture requests didn't come out of the blue; my trusting Grace to provide became a kind of mental aspirin.

Finally, one day in meditation I heard that once more I was accepting a half-truth. **To live by Grace is a definite possibility but it needs a compliment to make it a whole truth.** As I have often said, every truth at the level of human thought needs a compliment to make it work.

Yes, Grace would bring to me all that I needed at the time I needed it and the amount that I needed. Yes, Grace would provide the opportunities for me to use what skills I have. Yes, my life can be lived by Grace. That half-truth is definitely necessary and the realization of that half has to come before the other half of the Grace equation. It is like the First Star Key to love God, but I was not including the Second Key to love neighbor.

I, the physical and mental Walter, is my Spirit Self neighbor. In my quest for a life lived by Grace, I was not including the personal sense Walter. When I realized this I asked the Divine Process, my Higher Consciousness, for the answer to the other half it said, *"Walter you are the Grace you seek to live by.* **There isn't a power called Grace and you.** You and the decisions you make that shape your life are the Grace. The action you decide to take is the Grace you seek to live your life."

Of course, I am talking about the personal you who has conquered egotism, who knows that you are the Presence of God, the you that has no fear or desire for self-aggrandizement.

You, when you are impersonal about your personal self is Grace in action and the decisions you make are the Grace that you live by.

Grace, like all else in the *Double Thread* of life, is not either/or. **Grace is at once beyond your finite self and one with your finite self. You first surrender to your own Divine Higher Consciousness and after that take personal responsibility for your life and actions. It's all God.**

Grace, like Love, is energy and a subjective Cause, therefore an action of the Divine Process. Grace is the harmony of Love in action in and through our lives.

THE PROCESS JUST IS

The level of consciousness where fear, judgment, and a belief in the need for self-protection exist is created out of the belief in bad and good. As we talked about earlier, we must go beyond this belief, because without the kind of thinking which makes things either/or and separates life into exclusive areas there would be nothing but unity or oneness.

So it is this simple – if you can transcend judgments which categorize things in terms of good and bad, there is nothing that can keep you from realizing you are in the Kingdom of Heaven right now.

Now, we would all like to contemplate whatever will help us drop that bad or good syndrome; so we can turn our thoughts to God and what we think of as the Spiritual Path. But unfortunately, we have been so conditioned to think that God is "good" that unwittingly we find ourselves still trying to overcome bad with good, because where ever you have good you have the other side of the coin, and we are no better off than we were to begin with.

That's why I have come up with another approach that has helped me beyond belief – by seeing life as a Process I don't have to always like it but I can keep from judging it. **Likewise the Process does not judge; it is impersonal.**

The Process just is. When I say Process there isn't any connotation of either bad or good. Even the most died in the wool atheist admits that there is a process at work which makes the sun rise in the morning or which transcribes the incredible sequence of events over a nine months period which leads from conception to the birth of an infinitely complex living body. So, free from any sense of bad and good, we can contemplate the presence of a Process.

We can even call it a Divine Process without entering the realm of bad and good. **Then if we truly Trust the Process we can let go of judgments realizing that everything that happens is obviously part of the life process no matter what appears.**

No matter what happens at the personal level, and no matter how tempted we are to believe it is either bad or good, we can see it as part of the Divine Process. We can remember *Ecclesiastes* where it tells us that there is a season for everything in life, and rather than judge, we can Trust the Process despite appearances.

Sometimes it helps to look back on the past, far enough back to be free of present fears and judgments, then it is easier to see how each stage was part of one continuous process creating the person you are today, each necessary. Can you see how all the people who have been important to you appeared in your life through the Divine Process?

It can even help you forgive those whose actions have upset you, because not only were they brought into your life by the Process, but their actions were not personal, rather the way the Process has brought Consciousness into your life to be processed.

Human beings think they know when change is necessary or what perfection is, but human beings are bound by the limits of time, space, and a very narrow peephole vision of life. How could they possibly know what is bad or good in the long run?

The Process, however, includes the alpha and omega, transcends time, and is Infinite. It is continuous; it never stops. It was before and will always be. Sounds a lot like God, doesn't it? So, looking at it from that standpoint, how can we ever rely on our own sense of right or wrong rather than Trust the Process?

If we can Trust the Process and thereby truly eliminate the belief in bad and good, which is temporary at best, we will have learned what a life lived by Grace really is. **We no longer have to learn more, be better, or strive harder, because we know that the Divine Process is now and actually always has been living our life – and the life of everyone else.**

SURRENDER TIME

As long as Divine Order is hooked up with time it is a fallacy. Believe me, there is Divine Order and being fully surrendered to Omnipotence, Omniscience, and Omnipresence carries with it an understanding that the fulfillment of the belief in Divine Order has no date attached. Divine Order is beyond time, as we know it. Until one has a sense of continuity, that life is one continuous stream flowing ever onward, "infinite freedom," is impossible to truly accept. It is also impossible to "trust" that all is in Divine Order no matter what temporary circumstances occur in our lives.

What is Divine Order?

Divine Order is a process, which not only heals but also destroys what ever stands in the way of an unconditioned response of love and forgiveness.

In other words, as long as one looks for or equates Divine Order with personal sense, with material appearances, Divine Order is at best a mental aspirin we swallow to ease the pain of having to decide what is good and what is evil.

In order to truly know that Divine Order exists we have to be detached, similar to a parent whose baby is cutting its teeth. The parent is aware of the pain and confusion the baby is experiencing and yet the parent knows that within time or outside of time there is a Divine Process at work for the ultimate good of the child. That Process is Divine Order.

In order to surrender time we must relax in the flow of the infinite stream of the Divine Process. To do this, it helps to know that the universe is multi-dimensional. Time only exists in this dimension in which we are participating. Both matter and time are only real through our collective perceptions. **As we move into The Age of the Gods, we will surrender Earth time to cosmic timelessness. Divine Order will be seen clearly without our limited perceptions.**

EVOLUTION AND INVOLUTION

The soul is that part of you that is eternal. Your body, your personality, and your intellect all change, and eventually disappear from sight, but your soul, your essential essence, goes on. Each life time resembles a circle of birth to death, but in fact life is not only a series of circles each having its ebbs and flows but it also has a single continuity. The circles joined together become a spiral. Each journey from birth to death rising ever higher, until we finally ascend to the place where we go beyond the concept of personality versus Divinity. We, as human beings, are not only the products of evolution but also the result of involution.

The process of evolution and involution is the energy behind all life and growth. Without both nothing would happen and nothing would be created.

Take the atoms that make up a body, for instance. They come and go, and when the body dies the atoms that compose it separate from what was the body. In turn they reintegrate with other atoms and become a part of other bodies, plants, or things – perhaps flowers or rocks in their new incarnations.

Evolution is Creative Force moving outward exploring infinite possibilities of creation and expanded awareness.

Involution is that Creative Process of returning to the source, to essential Cause, basking in the All-ness.

Everything that exists in form undergoes both evolution and involution; they cannot exist without both. We like to think of evolution because it promises improvement and something new. We disdain thinking of involution because it looks like a step backwards and requires a breaking up of old forms or ways. But they are both the Divine Process at work.

A perhaps more clinical and materialistic explanation is dissolution and reformation. Physically, when "ashes to ashes" takes place, a body loses its shape and form. You could say it has dissolved into its basic substance, atoms. Then when those atoms become a part of a new form it has reformed.

We have to go within in order to let go and then move forward or expand spiritually. When that happens involution is taking

place at the level of our spirit/being. It is going within the All-ness of Consciousness where Cause precedes created form.

"Involution" is integral to the process that is necessary for us to become "evolved." When you are involved (involution) with something you become a part of that something. The atoms that become a part of a body eventually breaks loose and evolves as part of another body or form to complete the circle of involution and evolution.

Perhaps when one reaches the Consciousness of Infinity – ascension consciousness, where involution and evolution are no longer conceptualized – then one's soul is no longer on the wheel. Until then we had better understand the Divine Process both in terms of involution and evolution if we are to become aware of how the process takes place in our daily lives.

Equating the theory of evolution and involution as outlined in modern physics and science, such as Stephen Hawkin's big bang theory, isn't new – far from it. For instance, in a lecture made in 1896, Swami Vivekananda seemed to have anticipated Einstein's theory of time and space. He said that though life seemed like a straight line, eventually that line curves and becomes a circle – a matter of involution and evolution. Einstein didn't personally discover that truth, he elaborated on it. **By his own involution he turned within and dipped into the source of consciousness and out of that evolved for us the mathematical formula for the process.**

Today even medical science reveals that our transient physical substance is not our essential being. All the atoms that made up our tiny bodies as babies soon leave and new ones form a more mature body. Obviously we are not just material, we are not just those atoms.

The consciousness, that grew the body and which will one day disintegrate the body is the circle of life evolving and involving. We have to be involved in order to evolve.

This too has a double meaning. We have to be involved in order to evolve. **That is we have to be fully immersed in our spiritual consciousness, our Consciousness of Source, to expand as**

Consciousness in or out of form. You have to dive in fully to move forward.

This too is the application of the Two Star Keys:

The First Star Key is the realization that it's all God. To know God as unlimited, all-inclusive subjective Source, the One Power and One Cause.

The Second Key is the self-realization of The Presence of God as individual expression.

That which is processing our Being is our soul; our eternal nature that was never born and will never die. The body was born and will die or seem to die as it disintegrates, but the soul was never born because it was never material. It expressed itself in material terms, it evolved a material form and later involved to its essential consciousness, but it was never material so it was never born and will never die. Its individual consciousness continues.

Can't you see how that realization frees us from personalizing disease and limitation and how the possibility of spiritual healing is substantiated?

In certain Oriental religions it is understood that the Essential Self is Omnipresent because it, being what we now identify as consciousness, is not limited by time, space, or form. That would imply that in essence I am you and you are me because we are Universal Consciousness. Right?

That is true, but this is where I believe the Christ message differs from those who believe that after we stop reincarnating we merge into a kind of impersonal divine soup where we lose our individuality.

We cannot have infinity minus anything. Therefore my unique Being, though a manifestation of the one All-inclusive Omnipresent Soul, still has its singularity.

My soul and your soul are the same One Soul, but the soul is infinite and remains infinitely individual. You and I are an

individual presence in that One Soul, a microcosm of the macro cosmic soul, but, though individual, we are all that God is.

This is the *Double Thread* message that requires us to Double Think.

The reason the uniqueness of each individual soul could not be accepted until now has been because the capacity to *Double Think* had not yet evolved. Because we can now think two or more things at once, many contradictions can now be reconciled.

I can simultaneously know that I am God, Infinite Source, and that you are also individually God, the one and only God, and at the same time I can know that we are each singularly unique and also each other.

In fact, I must Double Think because only when I know that because of the process of involution and evolution I am now both an individual and ALL THAT GOD IS. As we move into greater awareness, double thinking will be a normal activity of Spiritual Beings in the next cycle.

THE PROCESS

Trusting the Process is applying the Star Keys to being able to live in harmony with the Universe. As our lives wander along day by day, we often do not see or feel we are in the flow of something beyond our limited sense of self, but we are. If we read our journals or reread the books we responded to in the past, we can see reflections of our consciousness evolving over the years. As our consciousness directs the flow of our lives, the journey travels both up stream and down, against the current or sailing blissfully along within it, as it. Yet the Process Itself, being timeless in terms of Infinity, ultimately proceeds toward ever-greater awareness and application of the consciousness of Love and Light. This is the natural Divine Order of the Universe.

Both in synchronistic moments in the now and in reflections on the overall flow of our lives, a larger Process is revealed. Some have called this larger Process "the Will of God", that may be, but we are each that will, free in our individual creativity to process consciousness into form. Edgar Cayce tuned into this Process as the **AKASHIC RECORDS**, which he was very clear in stating were not destinies set in stone, but were the probabilities of our lives that our soul processes spiritually through free will. Through the experiences of living this Divine Process each soul grows and adds to the development of the whole.

These records are not as pictures on a screen, not as written words, but are as forces in the life of an entity. 288-27 Edgar Cayce

Likewise, Quantum Physics has established that our consciousness creates our reality from the field of all possibilities. And as Lipton and Bhaerman explain in *Spontaneous Evolution*:

> *Extending (physicist John Wheeler's) notion to its logical conclusion reveals that no particular future is a certainty. There are some future scenarios that are probabilities and many more that are mere possibilities. The entangled field we all create with our collective thoughts influences all potential outcomes. What theologians identified as free Will really represents our power as co-creating participants.*

To Trust the Process is to engage in the Divine activity of creation as individual creators.

The Process is not a thing; it is a verb, an action of consciousness.

The Process surrounds us all every minute with possibilities of vibrational energy flowing this way or that, according to our own perceptions, thoughts, and actions.

The Process works regardless of whether we are aware of it or not, much less trust in it.

Consciousness is constantly creating. Yet without trust that brings allowing, the flow may be chaotic, bouncing one around here and there until there is a shift in consciousness that opens the Way to higher expressions of Love and Joy and Harmony.

By Trusting in the Process we allow infinite possibilities to present themselves to us as we hear and trust in our own inner guidance. Trust allows these higher vibrations to flow before us to make the crooked places straight. In other words, Trusting the Process allows Grace to guide our lives.

By Grace we are led to the Star Keys to open those new Pathways of possibilities in the web of life. **The Star Keys are clear and simple aids to traversing the rocky places and setting sail in the main current of The Process**.

Some of us have to search long and hard for the Truths of the Universe before finally getting around to applying them to our own lives. Many have to almost drown in despair trying to go against the Process of ever-higher vibrational expression before they let go and let life flow with Harmony.

The Grace of the Divine flow will ultimately turn us around no matter how hard we make it on ourselves in one life time or another.

Application of the Star Keys activates our ability to deliberately create our pathways through the river of the Milky Way as we speed along this new 26,000-year cycle.

It does not have to be hard. Nothing has to be hard, if we Trust the Process of Divine flow of Light, Love, and Joy to carry us forward.

If we Trust that we first know and perceive that it's all God, then allow this knowing to shift our perspective from the world to subjective Cause, then we can create and navigate the vibrational streams of life with ever greater awareness with Love, Joy, and Harmony. No rocky places stop the flow as we then sail along a vast stream of consciousness surrounded by our fellow souls, all One.

It is important to note that the Divine Process is not a map written in stone; it is a journey of cycles upon cycles full of endless possibilities. As Gods, we have free creative will to chart the course of our own journey.

We are not saying that to Trust the Process means to trust that God will carry you forward as an outside force or that this Process is predetermined by an outside God, regardless of our personal involvement. Even in quantum circles that propose theory to establish the existence of God, we are one with God Consciousness. We are a part of the Process.

God is Quantum Consciousness from which we are not separate. The Process is the creativity of Quantum God Consciousness.

> *God is the unconditioned agent of consciousness, the collapser with total freedom of choice that gives us true creativity. In our creativity we experience ourselves as the unconditioned quantum self, as the child of God.*
> Amit Goswami, PhD GOD IS NOT DEAD

In the new science of Quantum Physics, God is equated with Omnipotence, Omniscience, and Omnipresent Consciousness. Goswami also states that, "God is not separate from us; God is indwelling in us, in our consciousness. Consciousness is the ground of all being, which includes us." In his book, *God Is Not Dead*, he agrees that this God is not the traditional Christian God, but the God of the mystic, Jesus. He shows parallels with Quantum Physics and the more esoteric teachings of Jesus.

> *If they say to you:*
> *"From where have you originated?"*
> *say to them:*
> *"We have come from Light,*
> *Where the Light originated though itself."*
> GOSPEL OF THOMAS

The Light here refers to the Holy Spirit, the quantum self in quantum physics language. We have come from Light: our individuality is the result of conditioning. The Light originated through itself, through circularity, tangled hierarchy.

Goswami in **GOD IS NOT DEAD** *continues*:

*This Quantum God-Consciousness empowers the individual with its own free will, As above so below. This "empowerment" is the Process – the activity of creation, of Quantum God Consciousness in expression. **Or as Quantum Physics would put it, Quantum God Consciousness collapses possibilities from the infinite field of quantum possibilities we all are streaming through.***

With our own Divine Consciousness we can chose the course of our Process amid the ocean of Oneness in which we are all connected. We are always choosing our directions in the ins and outs of daily life. To better choose these directions, it is helpful if we know the Laws of the Universe which we will now explore.

Chapter Four

Truth & Law

LAWS & KEYS

When Jesus said that he had come to fulfill the law he was saying that he was going to expose objective law as a non-reality. To move into 2012 thinking and living, we must go beyond human concepts of law.

Human laws are created out of a belief in bad and good, as well as fear and limitation. Furthermore, they imply a lack of ability to live in harmony unless forced to do so. You cannot force someone to love his neighbor. You cannot force a thief not to steal because he believes in lack. Consciousness is what it is.

Raise the consciousness into higher planes of awareness, and human laws become a non-reality.

Jesus told us 2,000 years ago that there was another way – a way to live in the now at which time the belief in law no longer exists. Laws only exist by past comparisons or future expectations. Laws only exist because someone believes in a limited supply that cannot be shared with what they perceive to be separate objectified humans. We are fiercely defendant of our own self and our family on a personal level and of our social group and nation on a global level. We have not yet evolved into Global Humans, but we will or perish from the Earth.

As in the First Star Key, each individual person or situation is unique, and each is infinitely One with Source. Until this is realized in consciousness, individuals cannot see their neighbor as their Self, much less love all from and as Infinite Source, which is the Second Star Key.

People do not trust their own spiritual intuition, which is to say they do not trust what Scripture calls their still small voice, or what in truth is the Holy Spirit flowing through as their own inner voice. They think they need laws to create boundaries, rules, and uphold judgments. Because they do not listen, much less trust the Voice of Spirit, they allow social, fear-based concepts to live their lives for them.

In other words, humans create laws as substitutes for love of God, self-love, and love of neighbor. Not knowing the Star Keys, they try to control what is uncontrollable with laws.

Objective laws don't work – Star Keys do.

Laws are objective. They only deal with the effects not the cause. On the other hand, Jesus gave us a subjective law – Love. He didn't give us a check off list of things we should love and things we should not. He said to love everything and that meant to know the truth of everything.

It's our choice. Out of fear that if we do not make the right decisions evil will befall us, most people choose the illusion of law. Laws have held us captive for the past 26,000 years. It's time for inner knowing, spiritual intuition, and Grace to guide us. We can bypass human law and know it is all God. We can rise above the need for human laws with the Star Keys in hand.

Spiritual Laws of the Universe

The First Law

As we said, human laws are objective. They may stem from subjective intent, but they, themselves, are objective instructions to be followed if one isn't listening to one's intuition for the answer. **Spiritual Laws of the Universe are actually natural principles rather than rules of behavior or judgment.**

The First Law of Spiritual Nature states that one is never involved with person, place, thing, or situation but rather with their reaction to or how they respond to their consciousness of persons, places, things, and situations.

In other words, the first law is subjective, not involved with already created effects, but directs us to Cause. It places consciousness as Cause over effects. Because of this, Goldsmith and Einstein realized you couldn't solve the problem on the level of the problem. If the **First Law of Spiritual Nature or Being is understood and followed one is consistently living from the Spirit within and the outcome is more likely to produce the desired result.** This law of the universe corresponds to the First Star Key.

The First Law of Spiritual Being is that it's all consciousness. The First Star Key is it's all God Consciousness, One Divine Source of all. The energy of this key is Love, the primary force of the Universe.

It means for one to initially be aware of the Consciousness or Spirit involved with and symbolized by appearances rather than taking things at face value, i.e. the objective creation. The first law sets the stage of the true identity of the person as unconditioned being. Jesus said his first law was to Love God. Why, because to love God is to know that it's all God, all God consciousness, including our consciousness. To know that's it's all God is to know that all is Spirit, that all is consciousness formed. The truth of this first law was beyond the ability of humanity to grasp until these times of transition into the awareness of the next age. With this knowing, **Love is the energy of higher vibrations of Infinite Source.**

Before following the Second Law of Loving Neighbor, it is necessary to primarily see everyone as consciousness manifesting in form.

It is in the knowing that the form never leaves the consciousness that created it, that opens the doorway to love.

It is not truly possible to love neighbor as self, unless one knows it's all God. This frees us to allow love to override limiting judgments of human law. Human laws bind another to a fixed point of view that does not allow for a change in consciousness toward the flow of greater love.

As Paul said in the *Fifth Chapter of Second Corinthians*, when we do follow the first law, "all things become new," meaning that when we see everything as consciousness it is new, infinite, ever expanding. Before judging situations it is necessary to affirm that the number one Law of Spiritual Nature is paramount. To phrase it in metaphysical terms, **"There is but one power and one presence appearing as my life and the universe – God Consciousness."**

THE SECOND LAW

The Second Law, like the Second Star Key, is the double nature of consciousness. The love of God is subjective. Love is the creative force that is the All–ness reaching out to the invisible principle of life, the universal and absolute. **The love of neighbor is consciousness formed as the objective. It acknowledges individuality, specificity,** and material presence.

There again, Jesus gave us the secret. It is this priority. He said, "Seek ye first the kingdom of God." **Concentrate first on the subjective or spiritual nature of a person, place, or situation. When that is established hold it in consciousness; the other commandment is added, the love of the material universe seen through the eyes of Spirit as Spirit formed.**

A prayer, or any act in our daily life, must include both the invisible and visible. That way, when we first see the spiritual nature we can then look at the material picture in the light of its' spiritual truth, and the Word is made flesh and dwells among us. Then we experience the fact that it's all God.

The Second Law is that Consciousness manifests as form. Most importantly, form never leaves its Source.

God and creation are One.

The Presence of God is the I Am of everyone.

The key here is to first know that I Am One with God, that Self is One with all that is. Therefore when loving another, one is loving all – as Self. Jesus wasn't talking about *feeling* love for ourselves. He was talking about the reality that underneath everything else, at the core of our Being is our true Christ nature. When we can know this of ourselves, we can forgive ourselves our temporary limitations. When we know it of ourselves we can know it of others and forgive all temporary situations or appearances. We say temporary, because all objective forms change.

To love another we must first know the subjective truth of Being, which is again, the First Law. Objective human Love is fraught with limitations that rise and fall and do not last. Yet if we first know ourselves as Divine Being expressed as form, then we also know this is true of everyone. **As human beings if we cannot grasp the full depth of the First Law of Spiritual Being, then perhaps we can at least practice objectively applying the Second Law to how we live.**

To simply put it: ***Do unto others as you would do unto yourself.*** But you can't do this correctly until you know the truth for yourself. The Second Law will set you free.

> *Therefore for Humanity to move beyond objective law, these Laws must be known:*
> **To Know and Love God as All Consciousness**
> **I and My Father are One, All Consciousness**
> **To Love Thy Neighbor as Thyself.**
> **In other words, Love all form as Divine.**

The Laws of the Universe apply to all, whether we are aware of their operation or not; even though the majority still believe that life either "just" happens, or is determined by God. In either case there is little to no personal responsibility. This will all change as we speed into this new era. So let's explore some of these other Universal Laws and how they play out in our lives.

THE LAW OF ATTRACTION

In terms of Quantum Physics the Universe's Law of Attraction starts from the first law, stating that consciousness is the substance of all that is, then states that consciousness creates what is drawn to us. **We are consciousness, and through the forming power of imagination (image-ination) we materialize our perceptions.**

The quality of the form our life takes is determined not by what we think superficially but what we perceive as reality. Our perceptions manifest our reality. Our perceptions are how our consciousness operates within the body's biological system.

The Law of Attraction opens the door to realizing we create our own lives with our thoughts taking form, and that if one desires to change their lives they must change how they think. The Law of Attraction as it is sometimes presented in metaphysical circles only goes so far. Too often those who teach the Law of Attraction endorse a psychological approach to life, one that gives power to thought rather than Spirit. Though it is important to understand that the law exists, it falls short of explaining both the spiritual truth and the quantum mechanics behind the law.

The Law of Attraction can imply that we attract to us things that previously exist as though they are out in the world, apart from us until we attract them. **The truth is, as the beginning of the *Gospel of John* states, we start with the Word or idea and that Word becomes flesh.**

We create it – not attract it. This is subtle, but all possibilities exist in the unformed Infinite – unformed until we manifest them in consciousness.

Quantum Physics states that events happen from out of the infinite field of possibilities because of the consciousness involved in the event. Consciousness creates manifest form out of the infinite field of possibilities. No thing is separate from itself even if existing in different parts of the Universe.

Therefore you can use all the affirmations and positive thoughts you can think in your conscious mind, but that is still an infinitely small pin drop within your vast sub conscious. **You will only create what you are in consciousness.**

The only way to over-come old limiting concepts in your sub conscious is to know the Truth of your Being and dwell in the Kingdom Consciousness of your Super Consciousness. Our Higher Consciousness creates according to the highest possibilities accessible in the here and now of human existence.

The concept of creating rather than attracting is drawing a fine line of distinction, but this book is about clarifying the truths and not glossing over them.

Furthermore the Law of Attraction is energized by the Spirit in which we project outward and the emotion we put into our thoughts as we create. **If the Spirit is first subjectively loving, it will create**

in a harmonious way according to the highest creation possible. If it is not it will match whatever the lower, slower vibrations are. In other words you can project all day about having more money, but if that seed thought is charged with fear of lack, lack is what you will be creating. It is the same with sickness. Sickness comes from disease within our own consciousness.

It can be a very complicated matter. Simply put, if you are focused more on stress, anger, fear, and other debilitating vibrations, you will create the effects in your life and one form of this is sickness. We will discuss more about how this works in the next chapter.

The Law of Attraction is really the First Key in action. It is consciousness formed – Cause creating effect. You reap what you are. You can affirm all day long this that or the other objective thing is so, but **you will only create in your life that which you are in consciousness, because you do not attract anything apart from yourself.**

If you have the consciousness of lack, money may come to you one minute but be gone the next. You cannot attract something that is separate and apart from your own consciousness. There are no objective things out there somewhere waiting for you to magically attract them because you want to do so, or you say the words enough times, or you think positively. Sorry to tell you, it isn't going to happen.

It is fine psychology to understand the concept of the Law of Attraction, but one is not free if their concept of bad and good is in force. We, as our personal sense selves, do not always know what is needed or best for our growth. What we want to "attract" may be the thing that kills us in the end.

What is good? Good is only good if defined in terms of the greatest harmony for the whole. Good is not a lottery ticket, or a new car, or new relationship.

When we entertain subjective ideas or ideals, such as the belief in the possibility of having abundance, companionship,

or harmonious relationships, without specifically or objectively outlining the form we want them to appear in, your Infinite Consciousness is free to manifest in the best possible way.

In this new cycle humanity will evolve into putting first the consciousness of restoring natural order and expanding harmony for all before personal objective desires. The Law of Attraction will then be a vibrational delight for all. The Earth will abound in vibrations of Joy as we create from our own consciousness of Love, Joy, and Harmony for all.

THE LAW OF VIBRATION

The Law of Attraction in more esoteric circles is called the Law of Vibration. Several forerunners of the metaphysical movement spoke of vibrations in their early work, but soon found the audience needed more objective explanations and books were often edited when these ideas were too new to our human consciousness of the time.

I am convinced there are universal currents of Divine Thought vibrating the ether everywhere and that any who can feel these vibrations is inspired.
Richard Wagner, German composer and theorist 1873

The Law of Vibration states that everything vibrates and nothing is ever at rest and like attracts like, because vibrations of the same frequency resonate with each other. Everything is energy vibrating, including your thoughts.

Consistently focusing on a particular thought or idea sends out vibrations into the field. Your dominant consciousness resonates with like vibrations. We all have little thoughts, fears, and blips on the radar screen; they also send out vibrations but not with intensity of those empowered by our emotions or intentions. They act like bothersome static if not enforced.

All the universe is in constant motion – alive. This is the other aspect of this law, that Infinite Source is always expanding, always creating. Consciousness is ever expanding, thus all in the universe is in constant motion. **Vibrations are not objects, they are motion, energy in motion, the waves of the universe.**

Esoteric wisdom proclaims that in the beginning all things were created by vibration. The sound was the OM of Eastern mysticism and the Word or Logos of Western spirituality. OM and the Word were vibrations from and as pure consciousness – the vibration of God, or intonation of Primal Divine Source.

Divine Consciousness sounds throughout all creation through the vibrations of the music of the Spheres. Every form visible and invisible has its' own vibrational pattern or resonance.

The original primal OM is still vibrating as the humming of cosmic energy.

Science reveals that all vibrations have resonance with like frequencies. If you want to understand what you are "attracting" in your life, look at your core vibrations – the thoughts of your consciousness. The slower the vibrations, the slower and less harmonious the manifestations. Feelings of fear, grief, and despair vibrate at very low frequencies, the feelings of love, joy, and gratitude vibrate much quicker and are uplifting to all within their reach.

All the physical matters are composed of vibration.
Dr. Max Planck

At the very leading edge of biophysics today, scientists are recognizing that the molecules in our bodies are actually controlled by frequencies. In 1974, Dr. Colin W.F. McClare, Ph.D, an Oxford University Biophysicist, discovered that frequencies of vibrating energy are roughly one-hundred times more efficient in relaying information within a biological system than physical signals, such as hormones, neurotransmitters and other growth factors.

The Quantum Principle of Resonance states that a slower vibrational frequency will always raise up to meet higher frequencies.
Vicky Anderson, **The Expansion and website: www. hiddenlighthouse.wordpress.com**

What does this mean for us? It means that through the higher vibrations of Love and Joy we can raise up the denser frequencies of the body. **The higher our consciousness, the higher we can transform slower, denser manifestations. This will be of great importance in the age to come. Disharmonious thoughts create disharmony. If the frequency changes the form will change.**

The higher vibrations of consciousness contain mysteries yet to be realized during this new 26,000-year cycle. The Process will always flow by Grace to ever-higher vibrations. As we increase our awareness, so too will we raise our vibrational frequencies. Every thought is a vibration of subjective waves in motion that affects every atom in the body. **Healings will take place as we change the vibrations of our consciousness.**

Every life cell is thus moved and reaches outward to affect the whole of humankind. Healing sound vibrations have been used throughout human history and are being used even more as we grow in awareness. In this new cycle of the Gods, healings will be activated by vibrations – deliberate vibrations of uplifting frequencies that restore natural order in any system.

The Earth can be healed and restored to harmony with the vibrating of Higher Consciousness.   Imagine the whole of humanity in tune with harmonics of vibrations of Love and Joy! Imagine it in consciousness and it will be so.

Constraints from the past will vanish in an instant as awareness reaches pivotal numbers. During the progression of the next cycle, we will see spontaneous transformations across the earth and the whole of humankind, as individual and collective vibrations resonate with the frequencies of Love and Joy. Those following on the path will have the opportunity to make quantum leaps along the vibration ladder of conscious evolution. This will happen because there is no separation in the Universe.

I if I be lifted up, all will be lifted up.

ANOTHER LAW OF THE UNIVERSE
AS ABOVE, SO BELOW

As Above, So Below means that the same pattern is expressed on all planes of existence from the smallest electron to the largest star and vice versa. All is One. The inscription on the ancient Greek Temple of Apollo at Delphi was referring to this in the statement, "Know thyself and thou shalt know all the mysteries of the Gods and the Universe". Although amazing, it is more than merely the repeating of the key pattern of life. This pattern endlessly creates a correspondence between the physical, mental and spiritual realms that contains all knowledge and makes it accessible to all.

There is no separation since everything in the universe, including you, originates from the One Source, infinitely creating in infinite yet repeatable patterns. The writers of this inscription knew the Universal Truth, As Above, So Below – that the very structure of the universe is repeated everywhere.

An atom reflects the vast patterns of the solar system and infinitely, God is reflected in each of the parts. The Universe resonates to the same vibrations as does a single cell.

This is a holographic universe – a Conscious Holographic Universe. What happens in one corner happens throughout the whole and can literally shift the entire hologram. Quantum Physics has revealed that the universal hologram contains the original image or pattern of life in all of its infinite parts. This repeats on all levels. One cell of your body contains all that is needed to reproduce the whole you, whole and complete.

Perhaps the best actual illustration of this are the observations made by Benolt Manedlbot in his IBM lab. He saw beyond the apparent random chaos of the world of form into the world of the infinite creative. He discovered fractal images that repeat the "self-similar" patterns whether on a small scale or a cosmic one. Nature is not created randomly. Chaos does not rule.

Chaos is only the outer appearance of a Divine Process in motion.

Fractal geometry emphasizes the relationship between the patterns in a whole structure and the patterns seen in parts of a structure. For example, the pattern of twigs on a branch resembles the pattern of limbs branching off the trunk. The pattern of a major river looks like the patterns of its smaller tributaries. In the human being, the fractal pattern of branches along the large bronchus that repeats in the smaller bronchioles.
Bruce Lipton, BIOLOGY OF BELIEF

The Process that is consciousness in creative expression is One – cosmic, infinite, and non-local. This means that though you create your own reality, you are connected to the whole where each of the parts affects the whole. But moreover, the large Cosmic Consciousness of the whole affects individual manifestation and not by chance or random happenings.

As Above So Below implies that the Universe has laws that exist in the invisible infinite level as well as the finite material level.

We are including this law in our material because "as above so below," is a long established Truth that clearly expresses the key

Truth that It's All God Consciousness, above and below, within and without, infinitely and finitely. As hard as it is to imagine, all consciousness is within and without.

"Lay hold of me fully both from the within and the without."

An interesting result of this law is that although we cannot see the whole of Infinite Source, or even imagine all the possibilities contained in the creative web of life, we can see them reflected in our own daily lives. When we see with the eyes of God we can see the invisible subjective world in its visible parts. As such the visible becomes direct messages to guide us along the invisible path.

All of our creations are guidance from the invisible in the world of the visible. This guidance is received from the Infinite Wholeness of Consciousness of Divine Source.

We are standing at the door of a new paradigm in which we can truly live in the higher vibrations of Love and Joy and Harmony. We have lived for cycles upon cycles in slower, lower vibrational patterns where fear and hate set the tone. **The miracle is that now we realize we have the power of consciousness to raise these slower vibrations to change the whole. We are at the threshold of transformation!**

THE MUTABLE LAW OF COMPLEMENTS

Another of the basic laws is often overlooked or misunderstood, not because it is complicated but because of its simplicity. While we are still talking about the Laws of Truth, there is one subtle, but all-important, *Double Thread* prerequisite to all the others that is so obvious that we miss it.

Everything at the finite level needs a complement to complete it.

Note we said finite level, this then is one of the mutable laws, meaning they change with transcended consciousness, which we will explain as we go along. From our current perspective this law is often referred to as the Law of Opposites, or Gender. Because we are entering this New Age, we chose to call it the Law of Complements. As consciousness changes this mutable law is transformed into its true all-inclusive self.

But first let us explain how we get there. The word "complement" comes from a Latin word which means, "to complete." **At the level of the finite – the third-dimensional level of time and space, the "this world" level that Jesus talked of – no thing and no idea stands by itself. Everything needs something added to it in order for it to be made whole, to feel complete.**

At the human level, everything needs something to complete it. A right brain idea by itself is a half-truth, but when it is complemented by its left brain equivalent, it becomes a concept that transcends either idea alone. When our masculine side complements our feminine side and vice versa, we become something greater and different from either by itself.

In practical application, it is wonderful to have an inspired creative and innovative business idea, but if it is not complemented with a logical and feasible economic plan, it will come to nothing. All the business sense in the world won't make a success without the complement of a useful idea. Knowledge needs experience and vice versa. Knowledge that is not complemented by experience is fruitless, and experience is meaningless unless it is complemented by the knowledge of what has taken place.

From the beginning, the whole purpose of this writing has been to demonstrate how important and necessary it is for us to assimilate or combine the virtues of the traditionally objective, institutional, or material approach with the virtues of the subjective, intuitive, or spiritual approach. They are necessary complements to each other. There is not a single thought or thing, be it material, social, or spiritual, that stands by itself at the level of the intellect. That is why any statement that anyone makes can be contradicted. Speak any truth without adding its complement and its exceptions can be pointed out. One of the problems with our instantaneous society and quick-fix mentality is that we often do not take time to look for or add the complements to a statement that will make a half-truth whole. If there is anything in this book that you disagree with, it is most likely because we have unwittingly left out its complement, an addition that would make it a whole truth.

The science of complements may sound simplistic, but, in fact, we must be aware of its importance if we want to assure success and eliminate the last traces of guilt from our consciousness.

Failure to achieve our goal is almost always due to the fact that we have not asked ourselves what complement had to be added to our concepts in order to make them work. It is popular in business today to make mission statements, because in doing so, complements that are needed to accomplish the goal are often recognized in the process of objectifying the subjective mission.

Jesus included complements when he gave us two commandments because both were needed to complement each other. He didn't just say for us to love God alone. He added that we should love our neighbors or in other words, the world of effects as well. **Neither of Jesus' two commandments is sufficient to fulfill the law by itself, but when they complement each other, ascension consciousness is possible.**

Unless God (Love) is expressed in material terms, it is sterile, and actions that are not based on Love (God) are futile. Complementary wholeness is what James was talking about when he said, "...be ye doers of the Word, and not hearers only deceiving your own selves." Hearing needs the complement of doing, and doing is fruitless without hearing how to do what needs to be done.

As we transcend in consciousness, Complements are seen as the double nature of all expression of consciousness in form. It is the motion of the Universe, the Yin and Yang, forever intertwined as the circle of life. Gender is only a third dimensional concept that appears as two separate forms, or opposites. The soul is without gender, as it is all-inclusive and infinite.

As we move into the New Age the Law of Opposites becomes the Law of Complements, the double nature of one state of consciousness. **In its transcended state there are no exclusions, no divisions, no limitations.**

As Gods of the New Age we realize the totality of the Universe within our individual consciousness.

There are other mutable laws mostly of function rather than the immutable ones of Spiritual Being. They all transform into the key Truths of the Universe as we reach toward ascension consciousness in the New Age. The Laws we have presented here give us, for all practical purposes the keys to live a joyous, harmonious life if we understand their basic principles.

The application of the laws are the How To's of living a realized life in this next grand cycle. Words, laws, and theories are meaningless, unless we jump into the New Age with deliberate intentions to use the Star Keys and apply the Truths to our lives.

Chapter Five

Practical Mysticism

THE HOW TO'S

Practical Mysticism is the application of a state of consciousness that sets its priority in the subjective all-inclusive nature of the First Law and First Key.

With its timely *Double Thread* approach, Practical Mysticism applies subjective awareness to the practical side of living in the world. This section of the book is a blending of approaches, both practical and mystical, that complement each other in this new cycle. We firmly believe this is a pivotal time for us all to actualize our expanding spiritual consciousness. As humans we will evolve into the Gods of the Earth only when we master the art of Practical Mysticism.

The How To's of Practical Mysticism rather than being keys are more like guidelines or lists of instructions to use as we move into living in the Age of the Gods. It is not necessary for each one to be a key, as different ones may apply to different people at different stages of their journey. Besides if we had to carry them all around all the time, we would have a huge ring of keys far too burdensome to traverse the Universe. Travel Light and travel far.

So many people do not have what they think they want and are unhappy. But they do have what they have projected in thought, vibration, and imagination. Why weren't we taught the important Laws of the Universe when we were in school? Wouldn't we all have been further along the path by now? For sure, but it was not in the collective consciousness to explore why things happen on a deep emotional, or psychological, much less spiritual level. The word "vibration" was unheard of except in real esoteric circles, or scientific branches, and later in the song by the Beach Boys!

Consciousness slowly began to shift during the past two decades, but even as our customary concepts were stretched, our basic *modus operandi*, was still to act and react without much thought as to why or what we were creating. It wasn't common knowledge that we create our own lives.

Although we would never have called it superstition that is really what we operated under, as superstitions are beliefs and practices that do not follow the laws of science, i.e. the Laws of the Universe. Many religious practices as well fall right into that category. Our lives seemed to be buffeted around from event to event without much control from our own point of view. We prayed to a Godhead to make it not so, but that didn't work either.

Fortunately as the new cycle draws closer, psychology and metaphysics have explored the workings of the human psyche and why our lives are as they are. They discovered, or rediscovered the Laws of the Universe and put them into everyday terminology for us to absorb. Wonderful work has been done by people like Dr. Wayne Dyer to help us become more aware of how and why our lives are an out–picturing of our own consciousness. Dyer and many others attribute their shift in consciousness to teachings and teachers such as Joel Goldsmith, Mary Baker Eddy, and **A COURSE IN MIRACLES**, to name only a few. Esther and Jerry Hicks, through the teachings of Abraham, started many years ago to share the Law of Attraction and Vibration with small audiences that have now spread these "secrets" into more popular mainstream circles.

In my own life, I remember reading **A COURSE IN MIRACLES** just after Walter was given an advanced copy. He didn't care for it's wording so he handed it to me. I was not in a happy place at the time. We were still restoring the Guadalupe Ranch with the help of a group of artists who all lived in community. The ranch was a sure fire Mystery School where your soul led you when you had to deal with yourself, or else. In Walter's and my case, the Divine Process lead us to this mystery school because we asked to get on with it and become as aware as we could during this lifetime, so that we could help bring in what we now know are the Star Keys. It was a pact we made together before we came in to this life time and honored even when led in the dark by the Invisible Hand. The mystery was that we never knew where the Process would lead during those times of crisis and change.

So there I was insolated on a Hill Country ranch, surrounded by "others" I believed did this and that to me to create the unpleasant environment I was living in. I was not happy, wanted change, and opened a book that through the magic of the Process found me long before it was popular in bookstores.

As I slowly read **A COURSE IN MIRACLES,** page by page it led me to new realizations, that by the end of even the first reading had begun to shift my consciousness. I remember exactly where I was sitting, the feeling, the emotion, the realization as the shift occurred. Suddenly there was no one outside of myself to blame, all responsibility was shifted within. Yikes! *They* weren't the cause, *I was.*

It was so remarkable because that was the shift that lead to ultimately becoming consciously aware that there is no cause in effect, no cause in anything outside of my own consciousness; and that I could change my consciousness and change how my life out-pictured!

Walter has always said that you can't hear a Truth unless it is already in your consciousness, like notes on a scale. Now at this point in my spiritual journey the notes were in there, but they sure weren't playing any tune that related to how I behaved. Although I remember that shift point, it took a decade more before my consciousness changed enough to actually change how I really lived my life. Even now the How To's of living our increasing awareness is an ongoing practice – improved upon daily.

There is a very interesting part of this process that I did not appreciate until much, much later. It was that even as I began to change my life by changing my conscious awareness through diligent Mindfulness, Walter insisted he did not have to change, period, end of the matter. Oh, this was a major sore spot in our personal life. Of course I saw every fault he possessed and could do nothing about it. Nothing! And for those of you who knew us then, yes, it was a stormy relationship. Neither of us were very soft spoken either.

Slowly over the years, what I began to realize was that this too was a major life opportunity and again part of the lesson of the intense Mystery School we attended on a daily basis. It almost broke up our relationship until I decided that even though I didn't completely believe it would work, I would try what the COURSE instructed and Wayne Dyer and others began to write about as well.

That was to focus only on my own consciousness and what I choose to see in my life experience. It was time to take responsibility for my life. It was time to stop believing and start living from the Truth awakening my consciousness. The COURSE IN MIRACLES became my first experience in not only "how To's", but even in the need for living Truth in my daily life. The "how To's" started with how to change my consciousness to change my life experience.

We are creating everything and everyone in our life experience.

We can change our own perceptions and clear up those mistaken beliefs we have carried around far too long.

This is the only thing that you need to do for vision, happiness, release from pain, and the complete escape from sin, all to be given you. Say only this, but mean it with no reservations, for here the power of salvation lies:

"I am responsible for what I see.
I choose the feelings I experience, and I decide upon the
goal I would achieve.
And everything that seems to happen to me
I ask for, and receive as I have asked."
COURSE IN MIRACLE, WORKBOOK

Ha, that was easier read than done. As Walter and Joel would say, "You can't change a problem on the level of the problem." So first I had to change my consciousness to see any change in my life and how it appeared around me. It took awhile to make the shift to realizing we are the creators of our own life situation.

I know now that the greatest gift Walter gave me was to mirror every faulty concept and behavior I projected. A mirror I chose to see to clear my vision of myself; to know the Truth of myself and everyone.

It's so important to see interactions as holy encounters,
because this sets in motion an attractor energy pattern.
In holy relationships, you attract the collaboration of
higher energies. In an unholy relationship, the attractor
pattern exists, too, attracting low energies and more
unholy relationships. By bringing higher spiritual energy to
everyone you encounter, you dissolve lower energies. When
the energies of kindness, love, receptivity, and abundance are
present in your relationships, you have brought the elixir of
spiritual Creation or the love of the Creator right into the
mix.
Wayne Dyer, THE POWER OF INTENTIONS

Now must you choose between yourself and an illusion of
yourself. Not both, but one. There is no point in trying to
avoid this one decision. It must be made. Faith and belief
can fall to either side, but reason tells you misery lies on one
side and joy the other.

Forsake not now your brother. For you who are the same will not decide alone nor differently. Wither you give each other life or death; either you are each other's savior or his judge, offering him sanctuary or condemnation. This course will be believed entirely, or not at all...

Look on your holy brother, sinless as yourself, and let him lead you there. **COURSE IN MIRACLES**

The Miracle came; as I changed he changed. Yet there really was no change except in my consciousness, there no longer existed anything to forgive. He was right, there was nothing there to change, except in the falseness of perception. Regardless of where I was along the path, he held the Truth always in the Light. Regardless of what temporary circumstance we were experiencing in this human dimension, he always held the Truth of me in his heart. Regardless of confusions, and the unknowing of what our human mind thought it knew, a shift in perception gave the power of Mindful deliberateness to one who asked.

For in his heart there was always forgiveness that sees no mistakes. This is living as a mystic in the world.

For many of us this life time of transitioning between cycles is about living our deep mysticism in practical ways. We are no longer hermits in caves, or endless seekers of Faith. As emerging Globalized Spiritual Beings we are here to put into practice the Truths our awareness sees.

When I changed my consciousness everything in my life, appeared to change. Everything had to reflect higher and lighter states of Being. The Laws work, absolutely and impersonally.

Consciousness changes not by work, affirmations, or instructions. It changes organically, through willingness to step through openings in the "cloud of unknowing" to put on new concepts of knowing.

On the path of Awareness, there is a lot of letting go of

old concepts, faulty belief systems, and negative projections. Letting go is a constant process, combined with applying one's expanding awareness to one's daily life as the out picturing of one's consciousness.

Truth is only a "Half Truth" if it is not lived as the Divine Process of our lives.

We know it's a Process that can be trusted. It led us both forward into being kinder humans, which is the whole second part of the Process, the Second Key of loving neighbor as Self, in other words manifesting the Infinite Love, Joy, & Harmony of Source as one's life in form.

Even the activity of loving another is one's own consciousness projecting outward. Whoever is in your life is there because of your consciousness. If we can love Self as One with Infinite Source, then all others are included in this Self. How do we do this? Practical Mysticism.

Over the past few years we have realized several How To's that can help put your changing consciousness into form. In this chapter we share the ones we have practiced in our daily lives.

Our daily lives are barometers of our conscious awareness. You may think you are pretty aware and far along on the path, but look at your life, it's a tool to guide you. If your life is flowing smoothly in all areas, others around you may not be, so these How To's may help them along the path. We can all help make the crooked places straighter for those coming along behind us on the path as we lift ourselves up in awareness and apply that Truth to living on the Earth as Spiritual Beings.

FORGIVENESS IS FORGIVING SELF

Forgiving is an important How To, and perhaps a good place to start. It was a key for us both to making any shift possible.

The act of forgiving is similar to taking a psychic or mental bath. **As long as there is something or someone to forgive, one is not psychically cleansed of judgment.** To say that we must forgive seventy times seven, if necessary, is like saying that if necessary we have to take that many mental baths to be free of judgment.

What's a mental bath? It's cleansing our mind of false beliefs so that you can be aware of your Truth. **One cannot give from the Truth of oneself, if that self is imprisoned in judgments. Forgiving is the act of giving from the Truth of ourselves.**

In being forgiving, what do we have to give? Objectively we give some kind of present that shows how we feel, but that is not forgivingness. Subjectively we can give freedom from judgment. If we are not sure that we have released someone from judgments and thus forgiven them, the test is to see if there is anything we want from them.

As long as we still have something we want, whether it is an attitude or a thing, we have not forgiven that person. In forgiving, we release all including ourselves from limiting judgments.

Wanting is a matter of self-love. As long as we want something it shows that we believe we are not complete. It shows that we still believe that there is Cause in effect. Therefore forgiveness has nothing to do with another person it has to do with what we want from that other person.

The anger or hurt we feel when the need for forgiveness is present is purely personal. We are angry with ourselves for needing something, for feeling incomplete, for feeling we lack something. It has nothing to do with the other person. They are only what we are projecting our judgments upon to act them out.

The old statement that dependency breeds contempt is true. We become contemptuous of ourselves for being dependent on another. It isn't the other person that we feel contempt for; it is ourselves for being dependent. **And further it is ourselves we have to forgive for the belief that there is anything we do not have.**

We have to forgive our limited beliefs that linger in our consciousness. As we become aware of the First Star Key, the Truth of our Being knows that we are One with Infinite Source and thus are not lacking anything.

All possibilities exist. This can be a hard step to realize in our daily life. Lack, especially in hard economic times certainly appears to be real. It's a long process from conscious realization to step-by-step applying these principles to one's life. We certainly need forgiveness to help us move forward.

The How To of Forgiveness

Forgiveness can seem like a paradox, but cannot be missed. The first step is to let go of the idea that there is anything outside of yourself that needs old fashioned forgiveness. You are never dealing with person, place, or thing as Cause. Letting go of the judgment that holds you separate from your true self is the first step. Honestly letting the others in your life off the hook and shifting the responsibility back where it belongs allows them the freedom to be, and you the freedom to re-create anew.

Then forgive yourself! Hey, you only fell for the collective ignorance of our cultural world. **You can change your mind; you can shift your awareness to that of Spirit and live from Source.**

There is no blame, no sin, and no permanent act to chain you to your past.

It's as easy as getting up and being who you really are, living in the now of new possibilities. It started with you, and begins with you, so forgive yourself and move forward.

Love yourself as the Divine Being that you really are. To Love ourselves we often must forgive our objective appearances to allow our true essence to be "fore giving." That is to give first of our True self. The way to do that is to not react to those appearances by Trusting the Process – which is the only true forgiveness. Love is your highest vibrational energy. Sing with it. Dance with it. Live it, free of limiting judgments.

Love others by giving of your Love. True Love is fore giving, giving before asked, before need. And in relationships we must first Love Self then we can give of that Love.

TRUSTING THE PROCESS AS A TOOL

Perhaps the most important How To we can offer is to use Trusting the Process as a tool. To do this we allow Grace to guide us through the ins and outs of human life.

Grace is the energy of the Divine Process. We can feel it, we can hear it, and we can be moved by it. It is not only the voice of the Holy Spirit, it is the holy beat of our whole body, the feel, the emotion, the life force.

The Divine Process is guiding us to shift our conscious awareness into realizing what we are creating in our lives and in the whole world. Life on earth is the out-picturing of human consciousness. It just didn't happen by chance. Humans have created the problems we all are living with. **The goal now is to no longer go against natural order, but allowing ever-higher vibrations to flow through us as our own individual Divine Process.** By doing this we are in the direct current of restoration and transformation.

How do we know we are in the main flow of the Divine Process? **Our emotions are our guides.** How do we feel? Are we angry, stressed, happy, joyous?   Even if you get something objective that you want, how do you tell if it is the best possibility for your life? Did you manifest it out of Love, Joy, and harmony? Or was it manifested out of a state of consciousness that is less than Harmonious? How does it feel when you "have" this object?

Haven't we all gotten something at some point that we really thought we wanted, only to find that we didn't feel right about it afterwards? That's your still small voice, communicating as emotions, telling you maybe you are not in the main current. The way we flow in the current shows us where we are, what we are projecting, creating, and limiting in our lives.

Sometimes we have confusing thoughts about what we want. We might not know whether we want this to happen or something else. Do we move here or there? Do we take this job or that? **The How To is to Trust the Process, by allowing your inner guides as your emotions and intuition to show you what would be the best possible choice.** All of these inner guides are our own Holy Spirit communicating with you directly through Grace.

If you focus on what makes you feel the best, Grace will guide you toward the possibility that is the highest one available at that time. This How To requires time, the time to allow your thoughts and emotions to direct the path ahead. This is not a quick fix, or the instantaneous flood of reactionary emotions.

Sometimes we want to jump ahead, but we have to allow the Process to work for our highest good. **The Process calls for sitting in the silence of yourself and feeling your inner emotional stream, the vibrations of your heart.**

You have to allow yourself the time to feel these emotions and listen to your inner voice in the now, rather than operating out of past beliefs or collective programming. In other words, don't let the advertising media direct what you want in your life, or your family for that matter.

You are a powerful Being with all the guidance you need. Your deep emotions will reveal how your thoughts are matching your vibrations and what you are really creating.

Trust your Self. You do not need outside rules, judgments, social or political groups to guide you.

MINDFULNESS

Another How To is to be Mindful of your thoughts. Your thoughts form the projections that affect how you see others. Although our thoughts create what manifests as our life, not every idle thought will manifest; it takes time and space, and energy for things to appear in your life, so you don't have to traumatize your self over this How To. Too many fight against it as a strange Oriental practice foreign to Westerners.

Being Mindful is so important in being a practical Metaphysician it will be taught to you in many ways throughout your awareness process. **Being Mindful means to be aware of the Spirit in which we create something. The spirit we put into our thoughts infuses them with energy, quickening the energy of creation.**

To be Mindful you need to observe yourself.

What are your dominant thoughts? What are you putting the energy of attention on? The things that manifest in your life are the ones that have the most energy behind them, not necessarily what you desire. If your thoughts are full of stress energy and your attention focuses on the problems you see, you will probably create at least a certain degree of dis-ease in your life. If you fill your thoughts with what's wrong in the world, who's sick, what you think you lack, and other negative scenarios, that is what you will have in your life.

It may not be what you want, but it will be what you get. **The more you add emotion to your thoughts, the quicker these things will appear in your life, as your life. So the important thing here is to be Mindful of not only your thoughts but also the attention and emotion you are adding to them, in other words, the spirit infusing the thoughts.**

Being Mindful of yourself is a necessity for using the Star Keys, especially as we transition into this new cycle. It goes far beyond being an observer. Mindfulness draws you into your self-awareness, allowing you to know yourself, what you are creating, and where you are on the path of awakening awareness. It gives you the opportunity then to decide the direction and creations of your feelings, thoughts, and projections.

Mindfulness encourages responsibility.

Here's an example from my own life. During the period when I was taking daily care of Walter and writing on the book at a computer for many hours a day instead of doing outdoor activities, I had found myself slowing down physically. Mindfully I heard myself say things like, "I am tired. I don't have the energy I used to have. I'm stiff, my back hurts, I can't do that, or I don't feel like doing such and such." I heard it, but then I'd say back to myself, "Well, that's how I feel and it must be true, because that is what my body is telling me." Wrong.

Finally the words added up enough and I slowed down enough that I knew I had to change. Every time I started to say something aging and tiring about my body, I would stop in mid sentence, and listen to my inner Spirit. It was still vitally alive and full of energy. So I Mindfully began to change the tune. Since at first I didn't have the energy I once did, I changed the thoughts first. I would say to myself, "I'm getting stronger every day. I want to exercise and do the things I love to do outdoors, I feel healthier and vibrant." And I smiled, instead of allowing negative emotions to charge the thoughts.

It wasn't a matter of exercising to get fit again, because I didn't want to exercise. I didn't want to go to a gym or do exercise videos, or feel that "burn." What had to happen first was that I had to think healthy thoughts and regain the realized consciousness of a strong, vitally alive being. As I did, I could see things I wanted to do that I had not even thought about.

Suddenly there were garden projects and a desire to get back on the horses to ride returned. Life was good again. The garden and the horses were there all along, but I couldn't see them because my thoughts prevented me. It took Mindfully observing my thoughts so that I could shift the focus and create revitalizing ones. I added energy to the thoughts by smiling and joyously doing things I actually loved to do right here at home. **Up-lifting emotions helps us soar.**

Use the Mindfullness How To as a tool to observe your thoughts and what they are creating in your life. It is really only when you truly understand how powerful you are at creating the things that appear as your life experiences, that you will begin to be able to make a change. You have to understand the process and how you are playing the game.

Being Mindful isn't just about observing your thoughts; it is also feeling the emotional vibrations that are you. You are the creator, so observe yourself in your various human situations. Good feelings mean you are in the flow, bad feelings, mean you are cross-firing somewhere.

We cannot stress to you enough how important it is to be Mindful of yourself. You can literally use every minute and every situation as an opportunity to observe the power of your Creative Self. Every experience, from sitting in a traffic jam to talking with your friends, can be used to enlighten the boundaries of your awareness to see yourself clearly. In doing so you can allow the Truth of the First Star Key to fill your being. You can know you are One with Divine Source. You can direct Love into each situation. You can help transform the whole by knowing the Truth of your Self.

THE HOW TO OF FOCUSED INTENT

What you put attention on you create; this is true even of trying to solve a problem, get well, help a friend, or make positive changes. It can be a very subtle matter of focusing your energy of attention on finding new possibilities, rather than on the problem itself.

The more you look at the problem, the bigger it gets. **The more you look at the national news and put energy into all the problems they tell us about, the more they affect your own life.**

The media loves bad news because it catches our attention, and your attention adds to the overall soup of consciousness creating the events, multiplying them. **Turn off the negative attention getters, whatever they are.**

Say you are sick and keep focusing on how sick you are – pretty soon you'll be sicker. But you are not helpless to the negative flow you have created even though you may feel stuck on the problem that you do not really want. From this perspective you cannot even see the cure. This is why metaphysical treatments can be helpful; they allow another person to help you make a shift. They can't do it for you, but they can help you to know the Truth of your Being, then you can change from focusing on the problem which creates more problems, to deliberately focusing on subjective health and well being, which helps restore natural order.

When you are in so much pain you can only think of the pain, you might need a doctor, a practitioner, a shaman – someone to help you clear the playing field. At that time, some part of you calls in the help; that part knows the Truth and wants to be free of the negative vibrations.

There really are no separate people; we are all one in Consciousness. The Holiness of our Spirit speaks to the Holiness of each other. The mirror you choose mirrors your consciousness. However whether you seek intervention from a doctor or John of God for esoteric healing, the healing only heals the effect, not the Cause. **The intervention only temporarily diverts the flow of your consciousness. To create true healing, you must change your own consciousness.**

That said, we are very complex multi-layered systems with layers of consciousness and patterns of lifetimes all coming into play. If we saw the bigger picture, sometimes solutions may not be what we think they should be. **When we allow the Divine Process to work in and as our lives, we open the door to allow the flow of higher vibrations of greater good to appear.**

The important thing here is to focus on the solution in subjective terms. So if you are sick, change your negative thoughts, refocus your attention on healthy thoughts and see yourself healthy and happy.

There are cancer cells, germs, and all kinds of dangerous stuff around us all the time. They are triggered to attack us, because we open the door. We can help our bodies stay healthy by focusing intentionally on wellness, not what might happen or how sick someone else is, or even how bad we feel. Not only by focusing on wellness, but on being wellness. **This applies to any situation: first change your thoughts, and then create subjective uplifting ones allowing the Divine Process to carry you forward. BE the highest expression of your Consciousness you can with every breath.**

This is a very important How To – **first fill your consciousness with subjective thoughts of Love, Joy, and Harmony, before you project your thoughts intentionally outward. What you want to create from this Divine subjective state of higher vibrations is then empowered by the Infinite.**

It's not about manifesting a new car, a mate that fits an objective list, or any objective creation. **If we define our desires, wants, and goals objectively, we limit their manifestation possibilities greatly.**

It's all about Being and living as Divine Love, Joy, and Harmony in expression with conscious intention.

Here's another example from my own life. For months I had searched for the "perfect" horse. I was quite happy with the one I did find. On the very first ride out on the trails at home, something happened that had never happened before. I was riding along with a huge smile on my face, taking in the beauty around me and the feel of this wonderful horse beneath me. Suddenly, I was whirling sideways the opposite direction from the horse and saddle. All I could see was a flash of a baby deer as I realized I was too far-gone to recover.

Unthinkingly I blocked my fall with my arm. Yes, snap, it was broken. I grabbed the wrist and arm and sat there a minute or so, asking the Universe to bring in healing energies. I heard the clear inner voice of the Holy Spirit say, "Get back on now!" With invisible help, I was able to get back on the horse with one arm and get home before shock set in. I continued to call in healing energies and not panic, but this was a new experience beyond any fall before.

Well, the break was bad. With seven screws and a huge metal plate to fix multiple breaks, it took months to recover any use of the wrist at all. I had plenty of time to ponder the event and discover "why" this was not just an "accident." I got what I projected, right? Well yes, exactly.

What I realized was that I had been intentionally projecting so hard out onto the Universe to find a horse that wouldn't spook, that I was putting energy into the vibration of falling and getting hurt. Spooks are huge sideways jumps a horse makes when it is afraid. My own fear created more fear. I must have imagined a bone-breaking spook hundreds of times as what I wanted to avoid, but in fact helped create it by putting thought energy and emotion into it!

Unconsciously in that vast storehouse of the sub conscious, I had too many thoughts that I had ridden all these years without a bad break that would send me to the hospital, and I was afraid of just that. I was resisting the idea of a bad fall and being in the hospital to such a degree, that I added more energy into it than to staying safe. Resisting applied a huge amount of energy to that thought vibration. I was so *intentionally focused* on what I didn't want, I created it. My intent was focused on the problem, and projected it onto a previously non-spooky horse! I got what I projected with intent!

I know that if I had not been in such a happy mood, I probably could have created an even worse situation. Plus I know that the healing energies I did call forth created a process that led me directly to an amazing specialist. During the days before the operation, instead of continuing to project my fears, I shifted to creating a process of well being. And it worked; the special hospital he operated out of was a warm uplifting environment that was almost a spa instead of a fearful place I could have imagined. I was relaxed and totally unafraid.

After I realized I had carried the idea around about being overdue for a bad fall, then I could easily change the consciousness that created it. The shock and trauma of the situation allowed me the perspective to Mindfully examine my thoughts and the thoughts under those thoughts. It was a very informative process.

Thankfully, I was riding along in a more subjective state of joy rather than fear, so the Joy energy helped make the event not as life threatening as it could have been. **Remember it's not only our thoughts, but also the spirit in which we do something, and the attention we place on it.**

I did learn from the above process. I used the stream of thought of the process to reveal the how and why things happened as they did. I actually believe I gave myself this opportunity to experience my thoughts in action. In this instant I believe Grace guided me through a very long process of not only finding the right horse that would be safe enough not to kill me, but then guided me directly to an amazing doctor who put me back together so I'd have the use of my wrist again, and a hospital experience that was not frightening. More importantly, it allowed me the opportunity to increase my awareness of my own inner process and make corrections.

Needless to say, I am much more Mindful of the way my thoughts roll around in my head, and the emotions, energy, and attention I put into them. We do not have to learn the hard way! In fact, in this new cycle we can learn expedientially.

Instant Karma will be in effect, which allows us the real time instant ability to process what we are doing and creating, and change it by setting our priorities first on the subjective states of Love, Joy, and Harmony.

Being Mindful is being vigilant to observing your consciousness and being willing to change. Being Mindful is living in the now, as well as being aware of the ongoing process.

Awakening does require vigilance. Awakening requires that rather than merely going with the reactions of the third dimensional being, you begin to question, you begin to observe, you begin to feel, you begin to think more deeply.
THE WAY OF MASTERY

The important How To here is to Be Mindful of the power and content your consciousness, the thoughts it is projecting and the emotion and attention you are energizing them with.

Being Mindful will allow you the opportunity to use your powerful abilities to re-create anew. **Creating from a subjective state of consciousness of Love, Joy, and Harmony will produce greater results, even ones that heal and restore natural order.**

THE HOW TO OF BEING

The How To beyond being Mindful is being One with Source – alignment. To further clarify how we create and "attract" our life, we must finally come to the realization that all we have to do is Be what we Are in Truth. If you want a new relationship, first be the loving spirit that you are, radiate Love and Joy and that is what you will attract.

Disharmony cannot stay around you if you are aligned with Source and vibrating in harmony with the Universe.

If you want abundance Be abundance. This does not mean throw money around, or go out and run up huge bills. It means know you are one with Infinite Source. As such you share of all you have with the awareness that you are infinitely giving of Self. It's not an action of giving away or of piling up, it's being one with Natural Order. It's a state of consciousness that does not fear lack, because it holds no vibration of lack. There is no reason to "over do" just as there is no reason to fear. Balance and Harmony are in alignment.

Being in alignment is a state of peaceful flow along the vibrational river of the Divine Process. It's like tubing down the Guadalupe River with only the sounds of the water, the birds, the trees, all humming with cosmic music. Nothing exists but the now. **It is not a state of rest, because the Universe is always in motion; it is a state of resting in the flow. This flow of the Universe rises and falls, slows down and speeds up, all in natural order.**

Dis-ease often occurs when we resist this natural flow. Sometimes in our natural alignment our human self floats in a still part of the river, at other times races down the rapids. This is being in alignment. This is the Process. Perhaps in the silence of the still waters, we can reflect on our state of consciousness and explore possible changes. Or perhaps the Process creates a rough section of the river full of twists, turns, and white water rapids to draw dramatic attention to what is being created.

Negative scenarios can also be part of the natural order to keep us moving and expanding in awareness. This is still being in alignment as long as we do not resist whatever Consciousness is telling us. In alignment we listen to the Holy Voice of Self. Even a sickness can be in alignment as it directs us toward wellness. Every Buddhist knows life is impermanent. **In being One with Source, you do not judge any condition as good or bad, they are all temporary.**

When we are in alignment we are trusting the Process to carry us into ever expanding higher vibrations of Love, Joy, and Harmony. This means change.

Our journey in this new cycle will bring about changes. Our forms must change as our consciousness rises with higher vibrations of Love and Joy. Be not afraid. Be the flow – soft and slow, wild and rapid. Be it all.

The state of consciousness of Being is beyond fear. This is a very hard state for humanity to experience because we are so limited by fear within the collective consciousness. Change begins one soul at a time, one choice at a time. One moment at a time. The art of Being is living fully in the now. Enjoy the Process.

> *Things and conditions can give you pleasure, but they cannot give you joy. No thing can give you joy.* **Joy is uncaused and arises from within as the joy of Being.** *This is an essential part of the inner state of peace, the state that has been called the peace of God. It is your natural state, not something that you need to work hard for or struggle to attain….*
>
> *To offer no resistance to life is to be in a state of grace, ease, and lightness. This state is then no longer dependent upon things being in a certain way, good or bad.*
> Eckhart Tolle, THE POWER OF NOW

This leads us to the next How To.

DON'T RESIST, REPLACE

This How To is a very practical one that applies what we have observed about ourselves. **What we resist, we put focused energy on, which empowers our creative energy.**

After we practice the How To of Being Mindful of what you are creating, we then replace any unwanted thoughts with the Truth of your Being. We don't replace them with objective affirmations; we replace them with the power of subjective Truth. To do this you have to use the First Star Key as your Truth.

The First Star Key is the realization that it's all God. To know God as unlimited, all-inclusive subjective Source, the One power and One Cause

Resisting denies the power of knowing you are One with Source and blocks your own flow of Divine Order with slower, denser vibrations.

Whereas, replacing resistant thoughts with the energy of Infinite Source allows the creative flow of possibilities to open in your life.

By replacing fear based thoughts with the subjective Truth of Love, Joy, and Harmony, we are applying the Second Star Key to our life.

Every time we feel a twinge of a fear-based thought, every time we think about lack, dis-ease, anger, fear; Replace it with the Truth of our Being. "I Am One with Infinite Source! I Am Love, Joy, Health, Abundance, and Harmony! I Am God in individual expression."

The Second Key is the self-realization of The Presence of God as individual expression.

The act of replacing is the action of Spirit as individualized Self. This Self is the One Self that knows no fear from any thing perceived to be outside.

Replace, rather than Resist.

When you resist a situation you do not want, you put charged energy into it and actually attract more of the unwanted things by increasing the slower, disharmonious vibrations of what you do not want. Fear is the biggest charger of negative situations.

As we speed up our space-time lives entering this New Age, instantly your own fearful thoughts are reflected back to you. God Consciousness is ever expressing in higher, lighter frequencies, but will honor your creative free will of fear, even though it is a charged emotion that is actually creating the very thing you do not want. We have free will. Replace fearful thoughts with whatever you need to defuse them. Replace them with uplifting thoughts that open the flow of new possibilities.

The Lord is my shepherd; I shall not want.

He maketh me to lie down in green pastures: he leadeth me beside the still waters.

He restoreth my soul: he leadeth me in the paths of righteousness for his name's sake.

Yea, though I walk through the valley of the shadow of death, I will fear no evil: for thou art with me; thy rod and thy staff they comfort me.

Thou preparest a table before me in the presence of mine enemies: thou anointest my head with oil; my cup runneth over.

Surely goodness and mercy shall follow me all the days of my life: and I will dwell in the house of the Lord for ever.
PSALM 23

We are not alone.

Walter had an experience during a hospital stay several years ago in which he had to literally call upon the Lord.

Walter never takes pain or sleeping pills, because they tend to disorient him, but did the night after surgery. In a cold sweat he awoke in the middle of the night in a panic. Being Walter he got himself out of bed, wheeled his IV drip rack with him out into the hall to look for help. He wasn't supposed to be out of bed, much less walking. It was a quiet night with no one in sight, so he walked down the hall in a great deal of pain. About half way down the hall he knew he couldn't make it any further.

He had no voice to call out to the distant nurses station. He felt alone and about to collapse on the floor. With a surge of emotional yet silent energy he called out for help, "Jesus!" And in a flash he was revived and back in bed before he knew it. This is not a common verbal expression for him, at all.

When Walter says "Jesus" he knows that he means the Christ in individual human expression. He was not calling out to Jesus the man, or even God to save him. What he was doing was charging his emotional energy with the vibration of the Christ in form. He was linking himself up with the direct current of Christ vibrations to lift him up and get him back to bed.

The good news is that higher and faster vibrations can dispel lower, slower frequencies. This is a measurable fact of modern science. **Whereas, resisting thoughts can so block your flow of higher vibrational energies that you wouldn't even know a good thing when you saw it.**

The higher, lighter vibrations of God Consciousness are around you all the time; only you can block their transforming effect. The Lord is your constant Shepherd. Resistance blocks the flow. Therefore replace your resistance to anything with an open doorway to allow new possibilities to manifest through and as you in ever more loving and joyous ways. Again you do not have to define the how or what, but you must turn subjectively to Source to allow your highest vibrations to uplift your consciousness.

This means replace a belief in lack with God's infinite abundance. Allow the higher frequencies of infinite supply to flood you.

You have to have the vibrations of supply to attract supply, the vibrations of Joy to attract Joy, the Beingness of health to be healthy.

Remember, resisting magnifies the energy of creation into creating exactly what you do not want. Even in the case of illness, if you resist being sick, rather than to look at what your consciousness is trying to show you, health will not return until you change the cause. Resisting is a major cause of dis-ease because no matter what the situation, it creates vibrations that are not harmoniously aligned with Source.

Building walls around you for protection is resisting whatever fearful scenarios you are imagining. Every brick creates more enemies to defend against. **Walls, wars, or attacks of any kind only**

fuel what is actually not wanted rather than protecting what is wanted.

Resistance is a paradox of miss-creation. What is true is that you are One with Infinite, Abundant, Glorious Source. **The God Consciousness that created you, created you perfectly.**

What is our greatest fear? That we lose our life. The Truth is that we never die, life is immortal. Or we fear the loss of Love. Love is our natural state – it is constantly expressing everywhere. You cannot lose what you are in Truth. You are the Love and Light of the world, whether you know it or not. You may be blocking it from manifesting temporarily, but Love will override all fear as we move into the Age of the Gods.

You can replace any fearful resisting thought with Love. **To fully awaken to be the Gods of the next Age, we must replace all thoughts of separation from our human minds. We must replace fear with Love.**

> *That is not an easy thing to do; yet it requires no effort, save the effort to Love. Love is the great healer. Love is that which erases the imprint in the depth of the subtle world. The patterns that you brought forth with you as a soul are like a magnet. That is they attract the energy states in the physical dimension experience that are resonant with those patterns....Awakening does require vigilance.*
> *Awakening requires that rather than merely going with the reactions of the third dimensional being, you begin to question, you begin to observe, you begin to feel, you begin to think more deeply.*
> *You begin to replace what you would defend against with Love, Joy, and Harmony.* A COURSE IN MIRACLES

Withdrawing your belief in it can dispel anything you have created. You can replace fear with love, anger with compassion, lack with infinite subjective abundance.

When you apply the Second Star Key, you are replacing fear with Love and natural order is restored. What you do is to send out vibrations of Love, Joy, Supply, Kindness, and Appreciation from your alignment with Source, as Source.

A practical way to apply this How To is to replace even a slight thought that resists the positive flow of the Divine Process with a one that is full of Love or Joy. This works. I have used it myself to shift my thoughts and my creations in daily matters such as paying bills. When you write a check to pay a bill, instead of resisting the action by hating to write the check, replace the thought with, "Oh I love to pay these bills from my infinite supply, because I appreciate the service I have received. I love having free flowing water, electricity when I turn on a light," and so on.

When you have to pay a person for something, instead of worrying about the "lack" of money, or making the payment a negative experience that will create more negative vibrations in your life, think about giving loving thoughts to that person. "I love to give to you from my infinite supply." "I really appreciate how you have helped me and give freely of the Infinite supply of the Universe." This does two things, it shifts the negative flow to a positive one that starts creating more things to love and opens the doorway for infinite supply.

Now we know people in economic distress may have a hard time with this, but you have to turn the tide somewhere. And the only place you can really do it is in your own consciousness. Remember we said, **"You can't solve a problem on the level of the problem."**

You have to go beyond thoughts into the heart and cellular level of the very vibrations and emotions of your total being. By letting go of the resistance you open back up your natural flow of positive vibrations from Source.

You see anew with the eyes of God. The vibrant energy of Source is always there, but we shut down, block and limit the flow in and through ourselves.

It's like when you are stressed or worried, you clamp down the muscles in your face and head and the whole crown chakra closes to the flow of good all around you. You clamp down the spout of the vibrational field that connects you to the healing flow of Source. Whereas, the Knowingness that one is in Truth always connected and One with Source, allows the flow to heal, transform, and activate the process of positive out-picturing of your life.

If you can start living from the Truth of your Being that you are One with Source, ever higher, faster vibrations will resonate to attract new like vibrations of creation.

The How To is to replace any thought that limits your Being or creates disharmony with ones that are uplifting. The Universe listens to your every word! Your body listens to every word. Let go of the tension of resistance that blocks the Divine Flow.

Replace the energy of resistance with forward moving higher energy, and natural order will be restored to the way your life out-pictures.

How do we pray?

We need to redefine how we pray for living in this New Age. Prayer is not asking or requesting. **Prayer is an activity of Spirit, creating. True Prayer is the acknowledgement that one is already whole, healthy, loving, joyous, and harmonious.**

As we become aware of our Oneness with God Consciousness, the dynamics of prayer is reversed. **Prayer is a statement of fact, a command from Source as Source. Prayer is not faith or hope; prayer is knowing and Being.**

Praying to something for something does not work and therefore is not true prayer. Nothing is outside of yourself so praying to anything, even God will not change your situation. Prayer from a state of need only attracts more of what you do not want.

Your thoughts, words, vibrations, and prayers attract that which you are. Need attracts more lack. As we move into 2012 living as Divine Beings, prayer becomes our own creative activity.

Scripture says that your prayers will be answered if you pray aright. That is the catch. For most of us, the idea of prayer is wrong to begin with. It implies the desire to get something we do not think we possess right now, and as long as we put something in the future it remains in the future. You create the lack that you wish to do away with by believing in lack.

What then is right prayer?

Right Prayer is the fact that you cannot receive that, which you do not already have, in consciousness.

Therefore, prayer that works is prayer that infuses a situation, person, place, or thing with Love, Joy, and Harmony to restore natural order.

If a temporary situation seems to be out of order, diseased, or lacking, one can pray by seeing and knowing that these are not our true state, and allow natural order be restored so that one's true consciousness of the Infinite is realized. The temporary appearance of being out of order is only on this third dimensional plane; our consciousness is infinite and beyond limitation. Our consciousness is harmonious natural order.

We too often think that prayer is about helping Source to manifest something, such as healing, or money, or rain. We think we have to tell God that there is a lack or disease that needs healing. The fact is healing may come through dis-ease or even the temporary state of death of the body. Abundance will manifest only when we stop resisting lack and know ourselves as abundance. **God is Omnipresent, Omniscient, and Omnipotent and thus knows all timelessly.**

True prayer is about your awareness of Oneness with Source, perfect and infinite to be revealed by eliminating the blocks to what is already there in you. In doing so you let go of your resistance to a temporary situation. **Again it's a matter of replacing prayers that add energy to negative slower, denser vibrations with ones that totally affirm the Truth of your Being.**

Tell the Universe what you ARE! Whole, healthy, abundant, radiant, joyous, loving and the Universe will sing you up higher and higher.

Whenever thought is involved we are at the so-called third dimensional level of time and space. Our object in prayer is to experience our fourth dimensional consciousness. **Our prayers are our way of lifting our consciousness to an experience of the fourth dimension.**

So how do we pray?

Everything at the third dimension needs a complement in order for it to transcend limitation and become a reality. Creative prayer includes one's intention and one's attention. Intention is the idea – the Word. Attention is the action, allowing the Word to flow.

Dissect the words. Intention is an inner tension. It is subjective and experiential. It is the intention of allowing, of opening that which we have clamped down, covered up, clouded over. Attention is objective because it focuses on some thing. It is where your tension is "at," at-tension. One ignites the other. Prayer becomes prayer when that ignition takes place and the two become one. In that oneness birth takes place – the Word is made flesh. Intention becomes self-fulfilling prophecy when we pay attention to it.

Thus when we pray we set our subjective intent to allow our natural flow of Divine Order. That's it. We do not have to spell out the problem or the result; we have to allow the Divine Process to flow anew. In other words, we are not praying for something, not healing, not money, not help. We are allowing our own Divine consciousness to flood the situation anew. We are opening the doorway that we closed.

Prayer that works opens the flow. So prayer beyond 2012 in this next great cycle, is prayer without ceasing as our own Beingness. It is thought flowing vibrations of Love and Joy and Harmony, ever higher and higher. We are not focusing on something to happen. We are actively sending the flow of Love, Joy, and Harmony outward and trusting the Divine Process to move forward. Natural Order will be restored on earth for all, as we each make the shift ourselves to living from and as Source.

Prayer that works is not a request; it is an action, an infusing, an allowing, a giving, and a knowing. It is the activity of Spirit manifesting. It is Source flowing forth.

Simple, but to do this we:

First align with Source, with your True Self. Remember this is the First Star Key. This is the conscious awareness that you are One with Source that your life force flows harmoniously from Source, as Source. The platform this awareness sits on is knowing that it's ALL God. From this perspective you can view all life as One.

> *God is the embodiment of Truth and Truth is the foundation of the Universe. This Truth is beyond the mind and it transcends space and time. You must live up to this Truth and realize that the Divine is present in everything. Only when you can recognize the Omnipresence of the Divine, will you be able to experience God.* Swami Sai Baba

The second step is to apply the *Second Star Key*, to Be the Presence manifesting in form. Give Love outwards. Right Prayer in action is Love creating.

When you combine awareness with Being the Presence, this is 2012 living. Everything flows harmoniously from this state of alignment.

So Prayer is first aligning, then flowing outward with the action of giving of Self to All. It is being health, wealth, vitality, joy, love, and peace. It's about giving of your infinite Self. You are the prayer flowing without ceasing.

Prayer is an activity of Source, God, You.

THE HOW TO OF ALLOWING

Closely related to the How To of Being is the How To of Allowing. **To practice allowing, one lets go of limiting judgments and by doing so frees all to Be. It is the act of letting go of your own perceptions of yourself and all your creations.**

In the releasing there is trust and transcendence. Allowing is not taking in unwanted behaviors of yourself or others. It is knowing that we are each creating our own life and each on our on path.

You have to understand that Allowing does not mean we allow unwanted things in our life, it means we are allowing natural order to return to our life and deliberately open to the unlimited flow of Love, Joy, and Harmony. It's like the step beyond knowing when one surrenders to the Process with complete trust and openness. Allowing sets you free from the things that you once perceived imprisoned you.

It is letting go of the resistance to unwanted creations, and the allowing of joyous ones to flow freely. It is deliberately letting go of fear. It is deliberately letting go of your judgments you place on yourself and others. It is letting go of any feeling of lack.

Anything that is unlike the Kingdom of heaven is a habit well worth releasing by allowing it to be dissolved from your mind. THE WAY OF MASTERY

One who cultivates that ability to allow is cultivating, in truth, the very act of forgiveness. It is releasing the world from its insistence that its perceptions be held as right. It is releasing from the need to hold on to judgmental perceptions. Therefore, allow all things. **Trust all things. And thereby, embrace and transcend all things.**

A FEW PRACTICAL HOW TO'S

• I create my life from my awareness of my Oneness with God, Infinite Source. I am Whole, Healthy, Loving, and Worthy of the Infinite Good that flows to me.

• I deliberately create from my source of Infinite Love, Joy and Harmony.

• I am forgiving and allow all to Be free. I allow myself to Be freely All that I am.

• I do not resist the things I do not want. I replace them with things I do want. I do not fear the things that are whirling around me that are negative. I release them to dissipate and know that anything I do not create has any effect on me. It is a nothing.

• I set my intentions from my focused priority of subjective Truth, from the power of Love, the radiance of Joy, and the Harmony that sings the Universe.

• I practice compassion and kindness no matter where I am or in what temporary circumstance I find myself.

• I choose to see the world as a positive transforming place. I choose to see others around me as fellow travelers. I respect all things. My Self-respect is centered in my Beingness. I know this Truth of myself and all others.

• Everyone I meet is Holy. My body is Holy, my life is Holy, the world is Holy and we are all blessed.

• I begin each day with gratitude. I give with gratitude from my Infinite Source of Love, Joy, and Harmony all day. I bless my evenings with gratitude for a day of all possibilities, of wonder, and all that is.

• Gratitude sets the tone of my day as being thankful for all the blessings of life. Gratitude establishes subjective Truths as the Source of all that manifests as my life. Gratitude creates my blessings in the here and now.

- I am thankful for my highest good in the now, and in so doing empower my creations that they manifest.

- Gratitude establishes Truth in form.

- I am thankful that the Divine Process knows my highest good and manifests it directly and effortlessly out of the infinite field of possibilities.

- I am Grateful that I Am The Love, Joy, and Harmony that I AM.

- **I choose to Be That That I AM.**

Your beingness is the place from which your thoughts and actions come. When you disrespect your being, you set into motion a chain of reaction culminating in unfulfilled intentions. Wayne Dyer, THE POWER OF INTENTIONS

In this interconnected universe, every improvement we make in our private world improves the world at large for everyone. We all float on the collective level of consciousness of mankind so that any increment we add comes back to us. We all add to our common buoyancy by our efforts to benefit life. What we do to serve life automatically benefits all of us because we're all included in that which is life. We are life. It's a scientific fact that "what is good for you is good for me." Simple kindness to one's self and all that lives is the most powerful transformative force of all.
David Hawkins, POWER VS. FORCE

Thus as we move into this New Age with its accelerated vibrations of change, the living of these How To's become the stepping stones to true Spiritual Global Oneness and restoring the Earth as the Garden of Heaven.

Chapter Six

Global Responsibility

We are now stepping from being part of the problem to being the solution. The vibrations of change are increasing as chaos heralds transformation. What you are creating in your daily life is reflected in the soup of the whole earth. The new cycle calls for immense responsibility on an individual and global level. You are either a part of the global solution or adding to the world's problems created by the consciousness of fear and chaos. You can not separate yourself from the whole.

As never before, those of us who have opened to expansion are receiving detailed explanations in many forms concerning how to live as Gods in the New Age ahead. In this glorious Age of advanced awareness, both quantum physicists and metaphysicians know that our consciousness creates the forms of our life. In the Now our consciousness is creating instant karma as our thoughts pop right up before us and around the world. It is no longer a matter of slow evolution and dreamy manifestation; our life and our world instantly manifest as that which we are. We are in this together.

During this new cycle, who and what we are will be magnified in the out-picturing of our life clearer, faster, and with expanded intensity, reflected in the whole. Being stressed or negative at our core causes our vibrations to experientially attract negative situations to ourselves that we would not deliberately choose. More than ever before, it adds to the negative experiences occurring all around us. Think of it this way, as one with all humanity, you are responsible for every murder, bombing, or whatever horror fills the nightly news. Negative energy vibrations can not be heard around the whole world unless we resonate with them. We are on this path together.

Are you a deliberate creator of Love, Joy, and Harmony? It's time you are.

We can no longer act on our belief in separation of self or nations. We globally ravage our environment believing we are separate from our earth. We individually falsely believe our little transgression does not matter. It's wake up time, we are quantumly connected instantly. Parts of the whole steal from others, blind to the fact that the global economy is linked by consciousness and that causes us all to feel the effects of trouble in any area. Now, one comment made in one place can suddenly be linked worldwide and hatred, stress, and anger at others spread like wild fire.

The misconception of "disconnection" breaks down the natural order and the vibrational harmony of our world, both inner and outer.

On a global level our thoughts join with the whole to create vibrational patterns of love or separation. If you listen to the news, it's full of disconnections that spread inhumanity, hatred, fear, and disaster. Separation goes far beyond disagreement. It perceives the "other" to be a threat to one's personal self, and it eliminates personal responsibility for one's actions. Even listening to disturbing national and global news magnifies negative vibrations and creates more. Some how we have to stop feeding the dragon. Yes these are stressful times, but you do not have to perpetuate them.

We have to live our true subjective state of Love and Harmony to buffer what we take in and send out.

Are you part of the Global solution or the world problem? Where can you step forward to be more loving to others? Where can you share a greater awareness by the example of your life? Where can you replace negativity with Love? Where can you not feed the dragon? Everywhere you are, the grocery store, your job, in traffic, sitting alone in the dark, you are lit by your inner Light. That Light shines for all to see. That Light leads the Way.

True harmony resides in the Inclusive Heart. Building walls, bank accounts, and armies does not create protection. It only adds to the belief in separation. The Inclusive Heart does not live behind walls. It begins with each one of us raising our own conscious awareness and deliberately creating subjectively to align with the natural order of Harmony, Love, and Joy.

The Inclusive Heart knows it's Self as All. No one is excluded because of differences. Variety is the spice of life! This is a huge, monumental step for those who believe only their way is right and those that are different are wrong and separate from good, even separate from God. We can't change their minds, but Love can change their hearts. And it will happen. The Way of The Heart has begun.

As earth vibrations intensify, we are called to live with our Inner Being uncloaked. It is what we do individually that will change the whole. The good news is that human behavior is not fixed, rather it is governed by ever expanding consciousness, and the flow of that expansion is always toward Love, even amidst chaos. But the time is now. I heard the Dalai Lama say that we really have eons to learn to live as enlightened beings. True, we will continue to live as our own unique individual spiritual selves, but where? Perhaps not the earth. I'm not sure it has eons, unless it kicks us all out so it can start again in peace.

We have already received all the help we need and there is always more available as we continue to open to living as Gods on Earth. **We cannot have a healthy world if we individually are not examples of positive, loving, well being. It begins within each of us.**

The critical issue is that we have to begin to act consciously rather than subconsciously from old life threatening patterns. We want to be part of the solution rather than creating more problems.

Just as consciousness creates form, our emotions amplify our vibrational creations in the manifest world. Often our emotions are seen as barriers to spiritual growth. However, as we have pointed out, our emotions are very clear barometers of our vibrational creative path. If we are in the flow of the Universe, Love radiates from our Universal Inclusive Heart and we feel good – passionately good. Joy and Harmony are our natural states. Yet when we allow stress and negative vibrations to be created, we feel stressed, angry, and even sick.

So it's OK to let our feelings guide us and choose only to experience Love, Joy, and Harmony and let the others go.

We can deliberately choose the direction of our created forms.

We can smile even in the face of chaos and help make a shift, or compound the problem as we stress over negative scenarios. Living in higher harmonious vibrations deliberately and consistently is the solution.

We can refocus our intentions and make a great shift toward peaceful interactions, national and global respect for our diversities, and individual responsibility to be beacons of LOVE.

Start today by forgiving yourself and everyone. The act of forgiveness activates good old fashioned "redemption" by shifting our vibrations from negative patterns to positive loving ones. Forgiveness redeems your freedom to be yourself. The fact is you can not be Love if in your deepest heart there is a "but". In other words, that you could be more loving and joyous, "but" for such and such, or so and so isn't loving, or you yourself aren't worthy. There is no more time for "buts." There is no other, we are all One made in the image of glorious Infinite Source.

As forerunners of life in the New Age, we are called forth to live as Gods from the higher vibrational flow of Love that restores Harmony to all. The call has already gone out. Each one of us must create ever-higher vibrating frequencies that will heal our lives, our bodies, and our world. It's a 100% commitment. And it may well be an either/or scenario for the Earth and our lives on it; so let's do it. Choose to see with the eyes of Love and Joy and express from our true inner being the Harmony that resonates to restore Natural Order here on Earth. We are one with Source and thus are Love. Remember, *It's All God*. And Source is always expanding, recreating, transforming, healing, and loving.

Start NOW making deliberate choices to be living Gods expressing subjective Truths and thus, aligned with Spirit. **No matter what temporary appearance you have created, be all that you are, God Beings of Love and Joy resonating in Harmony with All That Is. Be it now, day and night.**

THE WAY OF THE HEART

We are now called to follow the Way of the Heart. This is not a new path, or even a new theology. It is the way God expresses as Divine Humans – as Christ Consciousness. **It is a way of meditating, of being, of living. It is a rising up and a giving forth.** It truly is the *First Star Key* then applying the *Second Key*.

In meditating on the Way of The Heart it came to us that as we rise up through the heart chakra the first experience is personal. We do indeed experience all the emotions and feelings associated with the heart but in this first heart chakra experience the feelings open to new possibilities of Love through our own Self awareness. After the third eye or spiritual center has been opened and the impersonal God consciousness associated with that center has been experienced a choice is faced. We can choose to use the energy to take us out of the body ultimately rejecting the world or we can reverse the direction and return to the heart to honor and love the world and all that is in it.

In the Tibetan system of chakras and Kundalini energy, Lama Govinda in **THE FUNDAMENTALS OF TIBETAN MYSTICISM** explains that we go through the chakras into the spiritual center in the head, but then do not continue out of the body. Rather we return to and anchor in the heart. When we set our goal as the attainment of a level beyond this world we are not only judging the world, but creating a dualism between God and man.

Our goal in this new cycle should be reconciliation where we indeed rise in consciousness to our full spiritual awareness and then see ourselves in that Light without excluding any of God's creations. It is the raising up to the awareness of the *First Star Key,* then centering that awareness in the pathway of the human heart using the *Second Star Key.*

When the second coming takes place, the second opening of the heart, the heart is filled with impersonal love and compassion. This second coming is also selfish, but this time it is the self with a capital "S", the All–inclusive Self. Love is felt for the Self of all humankind. The heart is the true center pathway of "As Above, So Below." The heart becomes the center of operations, even sending messages to the brain and throughout the human system. It allows God Consciousness to find expression, direction, and restore harmony throughout humanity and the Earth.

In their in-depth book SPONTANEOUS EVOLUTION, Bruce Lipton, PhD. and Steve Bhaerman, approach the Way of The Heart from a more scientific viewpoint. They explain how science is now confirming ancient wisdom, sharing such studies as that of Doc Childre's Institute of HeartMath.

> *Childre and a cadre of HeartMath researchers amassed data from a variety of new scan technologies that reveals the ancients were right in regard to the heart's influence on life. In their book, The HeartMath Solution, Childre and co–author Howard Martin concluded, "Heart intelligence is the intelligent flow of awareness that we experience once the mind and bodily emotions are brought into balance and coherence."*
>
> *HeartMath research confirmed what religion, poetry, and our own intuition have been telling us since the beginning*

of human awareness. The heart is the interface between consciousness and the physiologic responses that generate emotions.

Lipton and Bhaerman go on to reveal that, "the heart's influence on the field is empowered by its own electromagnetic activity that is 5,000 times more powerful than the brain's electromagnetic field."

Humanists who never achieve the impersonal level deny the power of spiritual love, and mystics who remain impersonal without returning to the heart reject compassion and deny that the Word is made flesh. In the new cycle both will be called to reconcile the approaches by seeking first the spiritual awareness of God Consciousness, then practicing and living it through the human heart where love is now the Love of God expressed all-inclusively and all-powerfully.

The third eye spiritual center and the heart center form a polarity. They are the complements of each other at the *Double Thread* level of life where everything needs and has a complement to complete it. When our energy flows from pole to pole and back again; then, just as in a light bulb, we are the Light of the world. This is the Light of Love that blesses the world. This is living the *Double Thread*. This is using the two *Star Keys*.

As Ghandi told us, "You must be the change you wish to see in the world."

SPIRITUAL GLOBALIZATION

The body is one and hath many members and all the members of that one body, being many, are one body. For by one spirit we are all baptized into one body, whether we be Jews or Gentiles, whether we be bond or free; and have all been made to drink into one Spirit. For the body is not one member,

but many. If the foot shall say, because I am not the hand, I am not of the body; is it therefore not of the body? And if the ear shall say, because I am not the eye, I am not of the body; is it therefore not of the body? If the whole body were an eye, where were the hearing? If the whole were hearing, where were the smelling? But now are they many members, yet one body. And the eye cannot say to the hand, I have no need of thee: nor again the hand to the feet, I have no need of you. Nay, much more, those members of the body, which seem to be more feeble, are necessary...And whether one member suffer, all the members suffer with it; or one member be honored, all the members rejoice with it.
I Corinthians 12: 12-31

History is marked by significant and evolutionary social turning-points that have created and defined the path to today. It is doubtful that all but a very few of those who were alive during those former transitional times had any idea how the future would be impacted as the result of the shifts in consciousness that were taking place at those times. Likewise, it is unlikely that more than a few in today's world will consciously realize that something profound is now taking place that clearly announces a spiritual and material transformation – a transition that will reshape life on earth in ways that are beyond and far more extensive than all past evolutionary changes put together. Also, despite the enormous effect this metamorphosis will have on our physical conditions, that which is taking place now has an equally unique and deeply rooted spiritual implication as well.

As we enter the Age of the Gods, a dramatic new advance in the evolution of consciousness has broken through. How long it will take for the forms of life to catch up to their potential is unknown. After all it's a 26,000 year cycle.

Like it or not, we are both physically and spiritually connected to everyone on the globe, and our individual well being depends on everyone else's well being, without any exceptions. Whether at a conscious level or not, there is a certain resistance to our facing up to our responsibility for world conditions. That is because it means we have to give up some of our own sovereignty. We, as well as our nation, can't be totally independent and simultaneously fulfill our responsibility to the whole globe. As one Global body we must work together as one Holy System.

As recently as fifty years ago the mystic priest, Teilhard de Chardin, gave us a warning when he prophesied, "The age of nations is past. The task before us, if we would not perish, is to build the earth." He was particularly prophetic when he included, "**If we would not perish.**"

Spiritually speaking, years before Chardin and others proposed the end of national boundaries it was realized that the world was a self-contained unit. The *First Star Key* has been known throughout human history. Although not collectively realized, being One with subjective Cause, God, if you will, the same Source unites everyone. We are all one body of humankind. **One body, whose essential Source is Spirit and whose manifestation is global; thus we are Global Spiritual Beings.**

Jesus' instructions for us to equally love both the invisible Source of our creativity (God) and also it's visible material manifestation (neighbor and self) meant for us to equally appreciate both Cause and effect. If we could love both, it would not only put an end to absolutes that exclude alternatives but also to the duality that divides. It would reveal that they were just different expressions of the same reality, the two Star Keys to living beyond 2012 as fully actualized Global Spiritual Beings.

Globalization is another word for Oneness and, despite material differences, spiritual "sameness." We can't have a total anything and leave something out. The Truth is not "either/or." It is about both physical uniqueness and spiritual unity. All people on earth have been cut from the same cloth.

In order for us to survive, Kipling's claim that "east is east and west is west and never the twain will meet," must no longer be accepted as true. Spiritually speaking, just as with our acceptance of both the east and west, we must now understand that we do not have a spiritual world and a material one. They are the same world seen from two different but similar and interrelated dimensions. No matter where on earth we live, no matter the color of our skins, or our current religious beliefs, we are all inseparable. In fact, if we study the world's different religions we will find that they all have globalization at their core. They all believe in the presence of a supreme power or Omnipresence though they call it by different names – Allah, Brahman, the Tao, or God. Every major religion includes the instruction to "Do unto others as you would have them do unto you," which is a fundamental global "how to."

As we have tried to explain in this book, the complementary "how to" that is required in order to make it work is the matter of priority. Up until now nations and individuals have placed results before Cause. The so-called bottom line has been a more important priority than what we have to do to achieve it. The objective or material approach has been primary, and its subjective or spiritual nature secondary.

The commission, "Seek ye first the kingdom of God," translates into the First Star Key – Seeking first the subjective consciousness of Love, Joy, and Harmony before imaging anything into objective material being.

If it were not that most people conceive of the word "spiritual" in religious terms, they would see that every action or thought conveys a quality of spirit, some negative, some positive, some loving, some not so. **Spirit is not objective. It is subjective, and the Spirit inherent in our intent dictates the characteristics of the results that follow.**

Nevertheless, rejoice, Spirit is at work. Like never before we are being drawn collectively, perhaps unconsciously, into recognizing our global Oneness. As we become conscious of our true Divine Nature, we step by step realize the Oneness of the whole human body. As the belief in separation becomes a distant memory, love for all will replace fear, boundaries will open, and love will flow without exclusion around the world.

Moving forward, we have to see ourselves as Global Beings, which means that we do not live in an either/or world. **We are both Spirit and form, subjective and objective, and when we learn how to make these two identities operate together we will have discovered not only the alchemists secret that turns lead into gold, but that the same all-inclusive Principle applies to the infinite nature of globalization.** The Way of the Heart is the key as it unites the two as one.

The answer is complex in its simplicity.

A global individual trusts the spiritual evolution that has brought us to an awareness of this Global Spiritual Consciousness, and that the evolutionary process will bring about the changes that will result in individual and global fulfillment.

As Divine Global Humans we will primarily see each other as the same Spiritual Beings that we, ourselves are, individually. Then, secondarily, we will continue to perform actions that will reveal the Heaven this globe is meant to be.

We will live forward knowing It's All God.

Facilitating the Shift

There are many who are now helping to make this shift, but we do not hear about their activities as much as we hear about all the depressing news the media feeds us. We have to focus on what we do want to create not on predominately negative news that helps hold that energy in consciousness. Positive up-lifting projects and stories help to shift awareness and be part of the solution. We can make a change in the whole by focusing on what we do want rather on what perpetuates more fear and hatred.

To make the shift we must use the *Second Star Key* to not only enable us to see each other as our own individual Divine Selves, but to honor each individual's particular Process. Esther and Jerry Hicks have expressed this beautifully from their teachings of Abraham as the *Art of Allowing:*

> *I am that which I am, and I am pleased with it, joyful in it. And you are that which you are, and while it is different perhaps from that which I am, it is also good....Because I am able to focus upon that which I want, even if there are those differences between us that are dramatic, I do not suffer negative emotion because I am wise enough not to focus upon that which brings me discomfort. I have not come forth to encourage conformity or sameness...*
>
> *...as you understand these Universal Laws, you no longer feel a need for walls, barricades, armies, wars, or jails; for you understand that you are free to create your world as you want it to be, while others are creating their world as they choose it to be.*
>
> Esther & Jerry Hicks THE LAW OF ATTRACTION

The miracle here is that as we raise our consciousness and begin to express Divine Truths in and as our human lives, we help to change the consciousness of the whole. But it all starts with your consciousness. We individually need to shift in consciousness to change globally. That consciousness is God Consciousness. The Process will lead individuals to groups, and groups to span the whole.

WE ARE DIVINE HUMANS
RECONCILING A DIFFICULT REALIZATION

As we speed toward this new age, our human perceptions are opening to the realization that we are One with God, that we are that I Am. Perhaps the realization comes in spontaneous moments of deep meditation where we experience the Presence as All in All, as Self – Oneness. Yet out of the meditative state of consciousness our humanity begs to differ and lays its personal sense of guilt on us, saying that we could not possibility be One with and As God. We could never say, "I Am GOD." Of course not, our human self only sees its limited sense of self. But our Higher Consciousness knows our Oneness.

This is a difficult topic developed in THE THIRD APPEARANCE and it still needs greater clarification. We will not be fully living our destiny in the Age of Gods in this great cycle beyond 2012 without the Consciousness of God Realized Beings. The cycle leading up to this era set the rocks upon the foundation of a temple 2,000 years in the building. It is the Way of the Divine Human.

Jesus was setting the groundwork, when he said, "I and my Father are One, but the Father is greater than I." However, in "Oneness" there is no superior or inferior. It has come to me that he meant, "I [my subjective concept of self] and my Father [my God Self] are one, but my Father is The Infinite, and thus more all-encompassing than I [my personal self]." As a wave, I am one with the Ocean, I have no end or beginning, yet the Ocean is infinite and knows its totality. In that way one aspect is separate from the other, whether referring to the human and the Divine or to our objective and subjective selves. This is a stumbling block many have never crossed; yet it is now time.

Today we are becoming conscious of the fact that humankind is as important to God as God is to humankind. **They are one and the same.** While this theory may be a shock to traditional religionists, it is the foundational belief that will lead us into the New Age of the Gods.

WE ARE THE PRESENCE OF GOD

Until we accept as fact that even with our human shortcomings we are individually the Presence of God on Earth, we will continue to maintain a sense of inferiority and it will be impossible for us to experience the glory that awaits us in the cycle ahead.

We must know and consciously experience this difficult step – that the consciousness that expresses itself as humankind is God Consciousness.

And further that because God Consciousness is Omnipresence, Omniscience, Omnipotence our consciousness is also. I know this is a difficult Truth. It's perception precedes actuality. The Mind of Christ has preceded us, Masters have joined this Mind, and set a well-marked trail through the Heavens as bright as the Milky Way. This path is the Way of The Heart. It is the rising of the Kundalini through our chakras out the Crown Chakra and returning into our Heart. Thus we are transformed by Knowing and Being.

Within each and every one of us is the *potential* to be all that God is. If we perceive it as fact, that potential will begin to manifest itself in stages until we find ourselves free of self-imposed limitation.

We are the Consciousness of God, and God is the Consciousness we are. When we *double think* and see our lives existing as a polarity between the finite and the infinite, we will no longer confuse the two ends of the spectrum. We will have solved the "crisis of perception" that has created the current state of chaos. We will live fully as Gods in the Age of the Gods.

RECOGNIZED POTENTIAL

By choosing to be born into the transition into the new cycle and to live beyond it, we must live God's Presence on earth fully realized – that is our destiny and our responsibility. We must respond to the God that is appearing as us and no longer deny that we are made in the image of that God. **We are Divine Humans.**

When enough of us live from this subjective Truth, we will have reversed the old priority that says we are first humans and secondarily spirit Beings, and see ourselves primarily as God's Presence instead of seeing ourselves as limited physical beings. Again, when the wave ceases to think of itself as just a wave and sees itself as how the ocean appears at the finite level, it is ready to take responsibility for being the ocean and all alive within it. **Thus when we see ourselves as all that God Is, we will be ready to be responsible for all living things.**

By the same token, it would be a foolhardy mistake for any of us to go around telling others that we are God as long as we still think we are primarily what we see in the mirror. It is unlikely that anyone who has experienced his or her Higher Consciousness, the I Am of their Self, would publicly make the statement, "I am God," because they would not want to confuse others with a half-truth. They would be aware that their human appearance was only a finite symbol of their consciousness and not the full, infinite, nature of Self that is God. Those who can see their identity or physical presence as a vehicle in the service of their Divine Consciousness, as the Livingness of the Presence, could legitimately claim to be God or an individual expression of God Consciousness in the presence of those who would understand what they are talking about, but not otherwise.

Spiritual evolution has brought us to the place where it is now possible to *double think* and know that when we say we are God we are talking about ourselves as Cause appearing as effect – as verbs appearing as nouns. **We can be both objectively aware of our physical selves and consciously aware of being the life Force that is activating our lives, without confusing our good with our Divine Purpose in life. This frees us to take our place as the Presence of God.**

To believe that our materialized human self cannot be seen as our God Presence denies God's Omnipresence. Such a one-dimensional way of looking at life creates the very ignorance it believes it is trying to eliminate. Perhaps it would be more understandable if instead of saying, "I am God," we were to say, "God is That which I am."

I used to cringe when I heard ministers proclaim, "Jesus is Lord." I don't any more because I realize that any man who could say, "I

Am the Way, the Truth, and the Life," knew he was the Spirit, or Consciousness, that was living in or as his body. If it is the Truth about him, it must also be the Truth about you and me. We will see that we are all God once we realize that we are the Life Force that animates our existence.

You are the Light the world is waiting for.

I AM MEDITATION

I Am the Light. In me there is no darkness.
That which appears in the world is an imitation of who I am and not the whole Truth.
I Am the Light of the World.
I have a body but I Am the Light expressing Itself as a body.
I am a perfect body just as I am perfect Light.
You see me, you see the Light.
You know God and you see the Light that I Am.
There is no either/or.
Where the Light is, there I Am; there is no dark. It is impossible.
I Am the Light of the world, all of it.
To be in the world but not of it, is to have a sense of humor about the human picture;
It is to surrender its temporary appearances.
Do not Resist, Replace all with Love.
The peace the world knows not of, is to be in the world;
Realizing you are not of it.
Peace is Gratitude's child.
Gratitude is the resting place in the business of life.
Gratitude is being grateful for being able to be grateful.

I Am the Love, the Joy, the Light of the World.
I if I be lifted up, all are lifted up with me.
I Am the Way of the Heart.

Chapter Seven

All We Need Is Love

LOVE!

There are as many different interpretations of the word "love" as there are people presently on earth, or ever have been. The meaning each individual attaches to the word has been filtered through that person's unique experience, and as there are no two people who are exactly alike, there are no two exactly similar interpretations of the word. Love can appear as an adjective, a verb, and a noun. The best way I can get the ball rolling for what it means to me is to begin by quoting from a letter I wrote to Eron, my wife on our thirtieth anniversary. It carries the authority of a true to life example.

"May the 20th

> *Dear Eron – my wife, my partner, and my love. You have done something that the dictionary could not adequately achieve! You have defined the word, "love" for me. I know that God is love; and that God is the word we use to identify the Creator of all there is; therefore, love is the Creator, and everything that has ever been created has come from that Source. As such, love is a verb, the verb "that makes the world go round."*

You have made me see that love is a noun, a verb, and also an adjective, which makes its intended meaning hard to pin down. As a noun, love is something lovable that has taken form and appears objectively. To the degree you recognize the Divine in another person, place, or thing, to that degree you love them.

As a noun, you are to me that embodiment of Love, Divine Love appearing as a person.

You are love made visible in human form.

As a verb love is energy. Teilhard de Chardin put it most eloquently when he said, "Love is the only energy capable of totalizing the world." Therefore, through your love, I feel myself more of a whole man, and as one cannot offer love to anyone else unless they love themselves, because of your love I am able to offer you mine. I can mirror back to you the love that you are to me.

As energy, love is also magnetic. It draws together those who have something to share be it rational, emotional, or sensual. That union can result in the generation of new beings or in the re-generation of existing ones.

As an adjective, it is descriptive. "I just love that dress you are wearing," or "what a lovely sunset", and, of course, "I love you".

God is Love; I Am the I Am that Loves you, unconditionally.

Thank you for the Love that I express as Loving you.

Love in All Ways,
Walter"

LOVE BEGINS WITH YOU, AS YOU

Walter has taught me two of the most important things in my life. First that's It's All God and that our first priority is to know and act from that awareness. With this awareness I was able to begin to see through the eyes of God to change my daily life patterns. It has been a long process with a long way still to go.

And after 30 years, he has helped me to know what it is to Love, not romantic love, but a Love that is inclusive, non-judgmental, and forgiving. There is no way you can truly love without putting your priorities straight. Another person is not responsible for your Love; you are. When I am love in expression, I am living the Way of the Heart and my life is transformed into daily joy and harmony.

During this process that has taken many lifetimes, we have both learned the true meaning of subjective love, forgiveness, and allowing. What a gift on this long journey. I have certainly come to know that it all begins with our own awareness. In these times we are called to be love in expression – Divine Love. **This is the only power that will shift the course of change to higher vibrations and restore harmony in our lives and on earth.**

Love begins with you, as you. We can't tell you how important this is, as both your individual Peace and world Peace begin with your Love.

In this new cycle as we put the subjective nature of a thing or situation before its objective appearance, Love becomes the new morality. The Way of the Heart becomes our highway to Being. If whatever you do is loving, it is moral; if not, it is immoral. All you have to know or do is to ask yourself if what you want to do is loving. How does it feel, loving or disharmonious; it's that simple.

Confusion arises when one mistakes desire with love. Love is not selfish in that it gives of its self rather than desires from another. No matter how cold you feel on the outside, if you feel love, there is an inner warmth.

In no matter what tongue, the most beautiful sound to fall on human ears or roll off the lips are the words, "I love you." Say it first to the God that you are, say it to Your Self, then you can say it freely to all.

God is not merely loving, God is Love itself and thus our very nature is also Love. From this natural harmonious state there is nothing to lose, yet there is infinite giving. There is no other that can take from us. There is no judgment, demand, or requirement. **True Love is unconditional.** This is the Love we are called to experience as we shift into living beyond 2012. The energy of Love breaks down barriers between individuals who realize they are not separate and leads to global Oneness.

Spiritual Globalization transcends ethnicity and religion, getting to the Heart of each individual. The Globalized individual is free of limiting judgments that would prevent True Self Love. The Heart is then free to overcome all boundaries, myths, and traditions.

When Jesus introduced the Two Commandments of Love, consciousness was expanded in an evolutionary leap of new possibilities. In this new cycle, we are ready for a shift in consciousness that brings that Unconditional Love into manifestation. This is the Way of the Heart. It begins with the self as the Self.

> *Love alone can unite living beings so as to complete and fulfill them... for it alone joins them by what is deepest in themselves. All we need is to imagine our ability to love developing until it embraces the totality of men and the earth.* Teilhard de Chardin

TWO KINDS OF LOVE

Just as there is Cause and effect, there are two aspects of love, one is the cause and the other the effect. Most often people attribute Cause to the effect. They believe that the expression of love is the cause of the feelings of love, that the subjective nature of love is objective. **Love is subjective, it is God Being God, therefore it is original Cause.**

Love flows outward as the primal energy of God as God. It is infinite and boundless. Because it is one with our own nature, we both inherently have Love to give forth and we seek the experience of Love in our human lives. The more we are aware of our Oneness with Source, the more we realize our potential of Love, the more we feel empowered, comforted, impassioned. This is our natural state.

When we feel separate from Source, we seek Love predominately outside of ourselves, because we believe we are separate from All That Is. We seek the second form of Love, which is Love in expression, but we too often do so at the price of forgetting Original Cause and think love is separate and exists outside of ourselves. The belief in separation creates fear. To avoid fear we seek love that is focused on objective persons, places, or things believing they will give us what we seek. What we believe we feel from another as Love is really only our own ability to Love mirrored back to us. Oh, I know that does not set well with a lot of folks, who insist they are loving and another is not.

Little do people realize that they are malpracticing someone when they believe that person lacks the love desired. It means they are seeing that person as lacking something, as being apart from God, of being primarily an objective personality rather than a Divine state of consciousness. On top of that, they may believe that another is withholding love because that person does not show affectionate love and does not show the human aspect of love. But Love is not affection. Relationships operate on many complex levels of human consciousness and awareness. Projections are bantered back and forth like tennis balls.

Love isn't really about how the other person loves you back. It's about your ability to know your own Divine Love.

Love of God is inclusive, impersonal, fore giving, respectful.

In the **GOSPEL OF RELATIVITY** love is equated with knowing, with knowing the invisible spiritual nature of another. We do not know what someone gives to another in terms of caring, inspiration, creativity, and so on. All we see, as human beings, is the external and whether it matches our interpretation of love.

Love does not judge by appearances. Love does not require qualifications.

To truly love another is to see their perfection and that their life is not apart from God's goodness. It is knowing yourself as one with Divine Love. **AS A COURSE IN MIRACLES** says, "Love sees with the eyes of God." That is one kind of love.

The *First Star Key* is knowing God as the Source of Love and setting this Love as your priority.

Love is an emotion when it is the *Second Star Key* flowing outward.

Love is a giving forth of your own awareness of Love in human form. Love is higher vibrations infused with energy, with passion, with emotions that guide the Process and restore harmony. Love is all we need to transform this new cycle into the Age of The Gods.

THE LENS OF LOVE

From time to time or at different stages of our lives we look at life through different colored lenses, from various shades of darkness to lighter and lighter ones, as we expand in awareness. We are taught not to judge by appearances, but if the lens we are wearing is distorting the truth our efforts fail. No matter how hard we try, moments of clarity ar,e few and temporary. Ultimately, there is only one solution that works.

Rather than trying to patch up appearances, the solution is for us to take off the old consciousness and put on a new set of glasses with brighter lenses. When that happens we now look out on the same life-landscape as it conforms to our new vision. We are now called to put on this new consciousness as we move into The Age of the Gods.

As our consciousness expands, the lens of Love becomes the clear vision of our humanity. Everything we see is seen through the eyes of Love. In this new state of consciousness, we know what it is to dance to the tune, "Love makes the world go round." And we can sing "We are the World" from our own hearts to all.

When I know that God is love I realize that love is God, and I am being Love – present right where I am. Love is omniscient because love sees the Truth in all that is. When I look at the human world without judgment of either bad or good I am totalizing the world, knowing that it is all one, and experiencing that it is all God – all Love.

Love is the air we breathe.
Love is the flower we smell.
Love is the light in a child's laughter.
Love is the resting place of our lives.
Love is the only freedom there is.
Love is the power of redemption.
Love does not need to forgive,
Because there is nothing to forgive.
Yet Love gives forth, unasked, without requirements.
Love is spiritual intimacy. It draws us to each other.
It wraps its arms around us. It holds us in its embrace.
Love is the nakedness of soul, unblemished.

Love is the Light of the world.
Shine it where you will and it will reveal
The Presence of God.

Heart-felt love is the gift you give yourself.
It is the fruit of your having loved.

Where your heart is there is your treasure.
Love is the Way of the Heart.

This is the new way for this new cycle. We must move forward with Love, instead of fear, lack, and separation. We have all read stories of unique people who exude Love. They are masters from many religions who so posses the ability to so truly Love that they attract us to them not because they do something, not because they heal us, or supply our daily needs, but because they consciously embody the Presence of Divine Love.

I once read such a story of an old Rabbi, who had to have caretakers help move him about, because he so loved each and every person he passed by, he was always stopping to smile, to embrace, to give forth of his Divine Love. He loved everyone. Everything he saw, he saw through the lens of Love. This is how we will all be, full of Love in expression. WOW!

> *All you need is Love. Love fulfills all things. Love embraces all things. Love heals all things. Love transforms all things. Therefore, remember well: you, and only you, can become the cause of your fulfillment, your peace, and your completion of time. This requires that you do nothing save remember to establish the connection with your Creator.*
> THE WAY OF MASTERY

Love is the Heart center of our soul and the beating Heart of the Universe. This is what we all seek – Love beyond words at the Heart of all Creation. As Divine Humans we walk the earth seeing everything as radiant Beingness. It is being in love with the trees, the rocks, the traffic, the crowds, and individual smiles that sparkle, not because of their appearances, but because It's All God.

Love is Joy. Love is Harmony. Love is all we need.

BEING LOVE

As we have said, **the Star Key beyond knowing it's all God, is Being Love.** We are repeating this, because it is vital to our transformation and the restoration and continuity of life on earth. We must set our human priorities to being the highest expression of God that is possible. **Simply put, our lives must become Love in action as we move into greater awareness.**

Inclusive, subjective Divine Love exists in our world as we manifest it into objective reality. This is what we are called to do as we live throughout the next great age.

Our subjective thoughts of Love will radiate outward to encompass the whole world. Everywhere barriers and boundaries that divide and separate will dissolve. Love will heal and restore all objective things to Divine Harmony. Perhaps the forerunners of this awareness have been the only things holding the planet together until Love can transform the world. The Mind of Christ has held the Light on the Path of the Heart for us all to follow. Buddhists monks have meditated on Kindness and Compassion for thousands of years. Everywhere groups and individuals have added to the blanket of Love that needs to circle this Earth and comfort each being. Today as we soar into this next 5,125 year cycle within the larger 26,000-year cycle the vibrations of Love are tuning up to raise Hearts to higher frequencies.

You are alive today; you are on the path. You have chosen to be a transformer. You have chosen to be a Global Human and you are Divine.

The life of a Globalized Divine Human is directed by a subjective consciousness with Love of All as its priority. Just as the higher subjective vibrations of Divine Love transform our daily objective lives, our human values become transformed by our intent to create harmony throughout the one body of all mankind.

Love is the vibration of harmony, the natural flow of the universe in perfect order. At present this harmony balances precariously on the edge of not only global economic disaster but on the fate of our earth, ravaged by global warming and fear based wars.

It is our job as Divine Humans to bring Harmony as Kingdom Consciousness here on earth, *As Above, so Below.* **In this new age we are Divine Humans with the mission of transformation.**

Divine Love is first and foremost subjective and when it manifests objectively it does so in ways that are supportive of Divine Order, in our daily lives, as a healthy planet, and establishing world peace. This Love does not manifest as buying presents to win love, or enabling destructive behavior, or enhancing one tribe, nation, or race over another. This Love does not fear itself, lack, or disease. This Love is not blind as it sees our deepest inner soul and knows how to lead us into ever-higher vibrations of an inclusive Harmony that dances with the Universe.

As Divine Global Humans we first see each other as the spiritual Beings that we are, which is Kingdom Consciousness, then take actions to live in the Kingdom. Again, these are the First and Second Star Keys!

The Kingdom might take a bit of restoring at this point, but God Consciousness is a consciousness of miracles and the earth can be restored to its natural divine abundance through the miracle of Love manifest. You, the reader of this book are called into action.

You are called to know the First Star Key – we are one with God, One with All that is.

As we set our priorities with the subjective consciousness of Love for all as All, *The Way of The Heart* **is opened for all,** *As Above, So Below.* **This cannot be just a thought that passes in and out of awareness it has to be our consciousness – heart and soul. It has to be the priority of our focus, our creation, our Love.**

Then as Divine Humans we are called to go forth and give of our Divine Self. This is the Second Star Key – To be God expressing Divine Harmony with every action.

We are called to Be Love, loving. We can then only create Love, Joy, and Harmony for that is what we are.

As we traverse the Milky Way, this 26,000-year cycle may seem incomprehensibly endless. In truth as we attain the knowledge of the *First Star Key* and apply the *Second Key,* time will vanish as a limitation. Our bodies will be transformed to vibrate to our higher frequencies. We will know ourselves as one Holy Body of Humanity. **We will know Love of Self for all Divine Humans.**

This Love will transform the Earth and restore it to the Garden of Eden, the Garden of Heaven on Earth, and we will live in Kingdom Consciousness.

It's been a long time coming, but to you all we can say, "We Love you all as Self."

Love in All Ways,
Walter and Eron Starcke

Let us all become the Way of the Heart and Light the World.
Amen. And so it is.

The Afterward

LOVE BROUGHT HIM BACK

In March of 2011 Walter had a stroke, which changed our lives immensely. Walter was increasingly homesick for Heaven as his body wasn't it's usual, vivacious self. It then became clear that we had to focus on writing the new book. Often to begin writing a book we would go on a tropical retreat to get away from everyday matters. He loved to meditate by the ocean to let waves of expanding consciousness flow. This time traveling was not an option. So here at home all summer I reread Walter's messages from the past few years.

It was daunting to read through all the messages and imagine how to compile them into a book. I've never written a book myself, although I have helped Walter on his. All I could do was to Trust the Process and allow it to move me.

What happened was a flowing of the *Double Thread of Truth* that has existed eternally as a bond between Walter and I. It wrapped me up and, without my mind being in charge, created its' Self into a book.

Over the years I have witnessed Divine Truth flow through Walter, closing the gap between his Divinity and humanity. It became our understanding of Trusting the Process. The Process led us to creating this book together.

As I reread his messages, I allowed Spirit to sort them and connect the sections. I became lost in the Process. Words filled in the spaces, up-dated lingering old concepts, and tied a *Double Thread* around everything. As I would read the pages to Walter, I found a new level of understanding had arisen out of the experience of writing the book. The "how" was through Spirit, the why was because it is in the mystical experience that true knowing arises.

It became an experience of listening and writing, then letting the truth settle anew. My consciousness evolved over the mystical Process. I am not the person who started the book. It is not the book we started. Originally Walter had intended it to be about Spiritual Globalization; it evolved into much more.

In mid July Walter seemed ready to cross over into more expanded realms of Heaven and explore new levels of consciousness. He called his friends to say goodbye. Hospice said he might not make it through the weekend; as he already had signs of physically making a transition. I had his favorite dinner Friday night, Chicken and Dumplings, but he ate only a few spoonfuls that I carefully fed him. I stayed close to him all night.

When he woke up Sat. morning, he wanted a cup of coffee and to my delight, to talk rather than drift back between dimensions. Since this might be our last day together, I wanted him to stay awake instead of sleeping most of the day and slipping away. So I fixed strong, caffeine coffee instead of our usual decaf. We talked and talked all day remembering our travels together and ones we will have through other dimensions and Universes.

As we held each other we spoke about our Love that was on such a deep level it kept us connected through difficult growing pains. Then we'd talk again about how I had to carry on the work, as that had been the plan since before we came in this lifetime and the reason I was thirty years younger. His new job would be to help expand consciousness from the other side, which he was ready to do.

As the hours rolled into the next day we were still talking about how much we loved each other and had learned and grown not only in consciousness but in how that manifests in our daily lives. Even when he drifted into sleep I stayed by his side, often right beside him in his hospital bed. At times he'd hold on real tight and say he wasn't going to leave unless I went with him.

Sunday Walter was often across the veil and about to leave this world behind. During the Process I did ceremonies as chants and mantras played in the background. As I lay with my head over his heart he slowly faded from this world. There were no sounds.

Then the Mystical Spirit took over, I felt his Spirit sweep me up and suddenly we were together in the Heavens with comets and whirling stars all around us. I felt intense vibrations of Light and Love. I actually thought we were crossing over together. Then we heard the words "The Star Keys, you have to tell them about the Star Keys!" He continued to talk to what I imagined were ascended Masters, as they were Beings of Great Light.

Shaking I jumped back into the world. I was trembling, sweating, and my head was throbbing. A few minutes later he stirred from his deep sleep of transitioning. He opened his eyes and said he wasn't leaving! We had to start over with the new book! He had detailed instructions about the Star Keys, we had almost forgotten why we were named Starcke!

Then he explained that he wasn't ready to let the Love go. The experience of Love as a Divine Human was worth staying here with me a little longer to set the memory in his soul. Our Love gave him the Life Force to finish his mission here.

It was Love that brought him back into life anew.

That day was so intense I was physically exhausted and emotionally drained. Interestingly a beautiful Christmas Cactus that we had for over ten years, suffered as well. For many years it flourished in a window that was now a few feet from his bed until that Sunday afternoon when it totally faded and wilted away. Later I was only able to save one small sprig to repot. The vibrations were so powerful, its life force had been drained as had mine.

As I took notes, Sunday evening the book birthed itself anew. Walter clearly saw that we were the "Starckes" because we were to spread the message about the Star Keys! We had not used this concept in the book to this point. We realized that this book had to be about the Truth in it's depth and simplicity – the two Keys to living as truly Globalized Spiritual Beings in this next 26,000 year cycle. Starcke saw that his many lifetimes had lead to this writing, as had mine. Our work had begun anew and would continue multi-dimensionally.

I have only begun to understand some of the things he said during that mystical wekend. He said he would clarify once he was on the other side, as his own consciousness was able to receive more. The Starckes would write more books. He did tell me how much my love meant to him and how important it was to him to know true Love on the human plane.   It gave him the strength to return to finish what we had begun with this book.

Starcke explained that he knew Love would be different in the other realms because of the differences in emotions and expression. He said that we'd always be connected as soul mates, but the love would not have the feeling or emotion it has on this earthly plane. He had not experienced this Love as deeply and now wanted to hold on to it as long as he could.

Love, true deep, abiding love is a powerful magnet and healer in consciousness.

When he decided not to go, we realized we had to start all over with the new book.

Love brought him back to share its mystical side.   Love brought him back to help clarify the Star Keys to living as practical metaphysicians in this new era.

Monday we were exhausted and could do little but hold each other silently. Thankfully, friends and Hospice arrived to help. They were all amazed to see him with bright color in his face, awake and talking. Tuesday I started writing the book as it is now. I, yet not I. His consciousness flowed through me as the Divine Process tied the *Double Threads* together as shinning Keys of the Universe.

I wrote, then read a few pages at a time to him so he could process it and make comments, changes, and smile brightly with agreement. We often didn't remember who wrote what, but that didn't matter, the Starckes wrote the book. The Starckes were fulfilling their earthly mission together, as long planned.

During this transition period it became clear that we should end the book with a new Chapter on Love. Yet Love is not an ending, it is the beginning. **From the *Double Thread* view of the Two Star Keys, Love leads the way into living as Realized Spiritual Humans. Love heals, restores, and creates anew.** Love is the Glory of this New Age. The Way of the Heart is the true straight path. We encourage you to Trust the Process of Love as your life in expression.

Thankfully we had three more glorious months together to share that deep Love and to finish writing the book. The week it was finished he started having little strokes again, TIAs, and again getting homesick for Heaven. It was the same week we were to have a long planned retreat to present the book. He was worried because he knew he could not speak clearly, but I assured him it was fine, I'd be able to conduct the workshop. And most importantly, that his Presence would be felt by all.

Spirit gathered a wonderful group to review, edit, and discuss the new book. By Sunday the last day of the workshop he felt well enough to have everyone come over and visit, have a meditation, and share a little while. He was pleased they all loved the Star Keys and so grateful to be able to see some of his dear friends.

The next few days Love again wrapped him in warmth, held him and let him slide gracefully to the other side of the veil as a mantra sung him to Heaven.

From the other side, he has communicated that he wants to be called Starcke from now on, his Heavenly name. And there will be other books as he already feels his consciousness filling anew and will communicate, as he is able. Meanwhile, I am to get out there and spread the word about the Two Star Keys to continue to do our part in helping to raise consciousness as we shift into the Age of the Gods.

Although after 31 years, I miss him, his Presence is still with me and I have heard him say, as he often did, "Have I told you today that I Love you? Well I do and always will."

I love you now and forever.
We'll travel the Star Ways together again.
Love, Eron

More to the story
The Starcke Statue

Starcke came into this lifetime to carry out a mission he knew well. There is no doubt we were together on this journey many times. Starcke was an old soul whose spiritual journey had brought him back to share with us the keys he had in hand. He will continue to share his consciousness to help us all transition in to this new Age of Being realized Divine Humans.

The following is a brief account of a dear friend's amazing realization. It leaves little doubt of the glory and mystery of the Divine Process.

My encounter with Starcke began, in this lifetime, in 1974 when I heard him speak on "The Gospel of Relativity". It was a profound encounter, although I could not at that time really understand all that he said! On that same week-end I was in an import store and, to my amazement, came across a statue of a monk that I knew to be Walter. My Starcke Statue has been my companion for these 37 years. At the time, I did not give much significance to the items he held in his hands except to note that keys unlock doors, mysteries.

I received his Circle letter, but otherwise had no physical contact with Starcke until 1987 when I traveled to his Guadalupe River Ranch for a retreat sponsored by Quartus Foundation. Walter came in the first night and sat at my dinner table. There was instant "recognition" and our friendship in this lifetime began. Over time we became aware that we had, indeed, had a life together as monks.

Through the years my Starcke Statue, often in my yard, faded and weathered. Over those years I gave less thought to the items in his hand. Then, in 2011, as Starcke's physical life began to fade and weather, I traveled to Texas to work with Eron and a group of fellow travelers to edit and discuss this book. On day two of the retreat, as we were discussing the two Star Keys to living in the new age, the

Light of connection went on and I called home to verify how many keys my Starcke was holding. Two!

This was a confirmation that, as quantum physics suggests, some futures are already probabilities. In 1974 the two Star Keys were already in his hand. Perhaps they have been "in his hand" since our lifetime as monks. This synchronicity also suggests that past, present, and future may exist simultaneously on the spiral of evolution.

When I sent Eron the picture of my Starcke (refurbished for the photo shoot), and asked if she had any idea what was in his right hand, she was astounded. "It's a dorje. He has one and he loved it because he said it was the original Double Thread symbol." Evidently the shape of the dorje symbolizes the two forms of truth, relative and absolute. "I actually had it as he was transitioning. I put it in his hand."

As he said, we do live by Love and by Grace. Trust the Process.

Good-bye for now my forever friend,

L. Darlene Pratt

BIBLIOGRAPHY

A COURSE IN MIRACLES, *Text and Workbook,* Foundation For Inner Peace

Braden, Greg FRACTAL TIME, *The Secret of 2012 and a New World Age* Hay House, 2009

Dalai Lama, THE UNIVERSE IN A SINGLE ATOM, *The Convergence of Science and Spirituality,* Morgan Road Books, 2005

Goswami, Ph.D. Amit, GOD IS NOT DEAD, *What Quantum Physics Tells Us about Our Origins and How We Should Live,* Hampton Roads, 2008

Hawkins, M.D, Ph.D., David R., POWER VS. FORCE, Hay House, 1995

Hicks, Esther and Jerry, THE LAW OF ATTRACTION, Hay House, 2006

Lipton Ph.D., Bruce H., THE BIOLOGY OF BELIEF, *Unleashing the Power of Consciousness, Matter & Miracles,* Hay House, 2005

Lipton, Ph.D., Bruce H., and Bhaerman, Steve, SPONTANEOUS EVOLUTION, *Our Postivie Future (And a Way to Get There From Here)* Hay House, 2009

Ralston, Peter, THE BOOK OF NOT KNOWING, *Exploring the True Nature of Self, Mind, and Consciousness,* North Atlantic Books, 2010

Stapp, H. P., MIND, MATTER, AND QUANTUM MECHANICS, Springer 1993

Starcke, Walter H., IT's ALL GOD, *The Flowers and the Fertilizer,* Guadalupe Press, 1998

THE DOUBLE THREAD, Harper & Row,

Teilhard de Chardin, P. THE PHENOMENON OF MAN, Harper & Row 1961

THE DIVINE MILIEU, Harper & Row, 1960

Tolle, Eckhart, A NEW EARTH *Awakening to Your Life's Purpose,* A Plume Book Publihed by Penguin Group, 2005

THE WAY OF MASTERY, Shanti Christo Foundation, 2005

A new message from Starcke from across the veil.

Dear One,
As never before I realize how Holy our Earthly
encounter is. It is to be cherished. Every breath
we breathe as a human is a Holy breath. The
ground we walk upon is Holy ground.
All of you who are in form for this transition
into the New Era have made a Holy choice to
participate in raising the consciousness of the
whole.
You were given this mission, carry forward: Arise
and shine, the glory of the Lord is upon you.
You all are the glory, the calling forth, the rising
up, and bringing forth of the Divine Human
experience on the Holy ground of Earth.
I Am with you, as are all the Light Beings who
have walked The Way of The Heart before you.
The Keys will open all doors.
I love you all today and forever,
Starcke

The messages of Walter and Eron Starcke arise out of the transformation in consciousness that is evolving as this new 26,000-year cycle begins. These are not the end times. This is the beginning of The Age of The Gods. This is the age of living fully and thriving joyously as Globalized Spiritual Beings.

As the Divine Process continues to lead us in serving this awakening Consciousness, new material will be shared. The Starcke's are still serving the evolution of Consciousness. Feel free to contact Eron.

For more information on:
Workshops, newsletters, speaking engagements, and continued material on how to thrive and live fully during this pivotal era,

Contact Eron at:

erons@walterstarcke.com

www.walterstracke.com

Eron Starcke

Guadalupe Press

P. O. Box 865

Boerne, TX 78006